MARRIAGES
of
JEFFERSON COUNTY, TENNESSEE

1792-1836

$\mathcal{M}$ARRIAGES
of
$\mathcal{J}$EFFERSON $\mathcal{C}$OUNTY,
$\mathcal{T}$ENNESSEE

1792-1836

Compiled by
EDYTHE RUCKER WHITLEY

With an Index by Deborah G. Sherr

CLEARFIELD

Reprinted for
Clearfield Company, Inc. by
Genealogical Publishing Co., Inc.
Baltimore, Maryland
1993, 1998

Introduction

EFFERSON COUNTY, Tennessee was erected on June 11, 1792. It was formed from portions of Greene and Hawkins counties and was named in honor of Thomas Jefferson. Dandridge, the county seat, was established in 1793. At its creation Jefferson County included what later became all or part of Hamblen, Cocke, and Sevier counties.

The first settlers came in 1783. Among them were Robert McFarland, Alexander Outlaw, Thomas Jarnigan, James Hill, Wesley White, James Randolph, Joseph Copeland, Robert Gentry, James Hubbard, Matthew Wallace, James Roddye, Richard Rankin, Thomas Snoddy, Parmenas Taylor, Hugh Kelso, Adam Meek, and George Doherty.

Among the interesting records of Jefferson County is one showing that on October 22, 1805 David Crockett was issued a license to marry Margaret Elder, who afterwards refused to marry him. The damage must not have been irreparable because on August 12, 1806 a license was issued for him to marry Polly Findley.

This present work has been copied from a register prepared by the Work Projects Administration. The WPA register was compiled from records which have since disappeared from the courthouse, so for the early period of the county's history the register offers the only evidence of marriage. Its value to the genealogist is therefore considerable, even though it must be regarded as a secondary source.

Edythe Rucker Whitley
Nashville, Tennessee

JEFFERSON COUNTY, TENNESSEE

Marriages, 1792-1836

1	No date	Andrew Cowan to Jean Walker
2	Dec. 25, 1792	John Paget to Elizabeth Leth
3	Dec. 27, 1792	Joseph Thomas to Polly Wright
4	Oct. 9, 1792	Jonathan Hill to Jenny Hunter
5	Dec. 24, 1792	Joseph Langdon to Katherine S. Fitsgerald
6	Sept. 22, 1792	John Hays to Mary Perry
7	Oct. __, 1792	Edward Clingham to Jennet Kinkaid
8	Dec. 26, 1792	Joseph Thompson to Ann Rogers
9	Dec. 2, 1792	Walter Evans to Lena Murphy
10	Dec. 2, 1792	Wm. Garret to Elizabeth Roulstone
11	July 26, 1792	Clark Thornton to _____
12	Aug. 30, 1792	George Waddle to _____
13	July 24, 1792	Andrew Bryan to _____
14	July 26, 1792	John Anderson to _____
15	Dec. 23, 1792	Andrew Edgar to Jenny Henderson
16	Mar. 20, 1793	William Allen to Mary Copeland
17	Feb. 1, 1793	John Giger to Susannah Creeks
18	Feb. 11, 1793	Benjamine Allen to Elizabeth David
19	Nov. 5, 1793	Major Lea to Levina Jarnagin
20	Oct. 1, 1793	Thomas Hill to Molly Tillny
21	Jan. 29, 1793	Malachi Howell to Elizabeth Reedy
22	Dec. 21, 1793	James Campbell to Jenny Ellis
23	Dec. 24, 1793	John Inman to Ann Shelton
24	March 9, 1793	Chesley Jarnigan to Martha Barton
25	Jan. 23, 1793	Elias Davis to Lidia Smith
26	Feb. 26, 1793	Simon Smith to Sarah Austin
27	Feb. 27, 1793	Hugh Kilpatrick to Ruth Samples
28	Jan. 5, 1793	George McFarlin to Sally Jack
29	April 8, 1793	Solimon Yoken to Susannah Adams
30	April 1, 1793	James Harden Jr. to Eleanor Gooden
31	Oct. 2, 1793	Gideon Blackburn to Grizzy Blackburn
32	Dec. 20, 1793	James Farrell to Hansey Miller
33	May 14, 1793	Wm. Provine to Rachel Cooper
34	April 24, 1793	John Cofman to Ann Shanks
35	May 4, 1793	William Britain to Fanny King
36	Jan. 23, 1793	Thomas Brown to Selvy Hask
37	Nov. 14, 1793	Wm. McMahon to Ellis Russell

38	Dec. 27, 17...	Josiah Leath to Rachel Doherty
39	Feb. 13, 1793	John Edwards to Elizabeth Soliman
40	Feb. 19, 1793	Geo. Galliher to Sallie Oaks
41	Jan. 30, 1793	John Brown to Sarah Gest
42	April 24, 1794	Solimon Copeland to Rebecca Davis
43	June 21, 1794	Eli Hargrave to Juda Hackley
44	July 3, 1794	Samuel McRoberts to Mary Snodgrass
45	Nov. 7, 1794	James Anderton to Peggy Morris
46	Jan. 14, 1794	Jesse Bird to Sally Rentfro
47	May 16, 1794	William Samples to Margaret Sterling
48	Dec. 30, 1794	David Herbert to Polly Fitzgerald
49	Aug. 1, 1794	John Williams to Peggy Renne
50	Aug. 12, 1794	John Dodson to Isabelle Johnson
51	May 10, 1794	Peter Looney to Mary Sharp
52	Nov. 4, 1794	James McCoy to Anne Gayley
53	Jan. 31, 1794	James Lester to Betsey Witt
54	Feb. 10, 1794	George Renno to Jean Reed
55	Aug. 27, 1794	James Garrison to Mary Grissom
56	Aug. 12, 1794	John Denniston to Pheobe Williams
57	Sept. 20, 1794	Henry Thornburgh to Ann Molsby
58	Aug. 23, 1794	John McGhee to Ester Glendenan
59	Feb. 13, 1794	James Doherty to Jim Cowan
60	___	C. Collins to Elizabeth Buckingham
61	May 3, 1794	Noah Witt to Millie Maize
62	March 18, 1794	David Beyless to Rachel West
63	Aug. 19, 1794	George Williams to Mary Johnson
64	Dec. 19, 1794	Nathan Thompson to Elizabeth Weaver
65	July 5, 1794	Wm. Shields to Agnes Creswell
66	Feb. 13, 1794	Allen Williams to Jean Woodard
67	Jan. 7, 1794	Isaac Cofman to Amery Carson
68	Feb. 19, 1794	William Campbell to M. King
69	May 6, 1794	Christopher Bullard to Rachael Fitzhgerald
70	June 18, 1794	Andrew Kerr to Katherine Sterling
71	Jan. 4, 1794	Aron Slover to Elizabeth Hill
72	Dec. 17, 1794	Solimon Aldred to Mary McDonald
73	Aug. 10, 1794	Thomas McCogg to Sarah Oliver
74	Sept. 2, 1874 (1774)	Joseph Henderson to Polly White
75	June 26, 1795	David Hoin to Priscilla Jarnagin
76	Jan. 14, 1794	Richard Woods to Fanny Libarger
77	Sept. 6, 1795	William Roulstone to Ann Moore
78	Oct. 28, 1795	John Moffett to ___ Cox
79	Aug. 5, 1795	John Dean to Jeligh Fowler
80	Aug. 5, 1795	Wm. Cox to Mary Neile
81	Dec. 19, 1795	William Milliken to Hannah Brazelton
82	Dec. 19, 1795	John Mills to Charity Mandenhall

JEFFERSON COUNTY MARRIAGES

83	Aug. 19, 1795	Patrick Morris to Elender Lea
84	Aug. 4, 1795	Duke Kimbro to Unnis Carlock
85	Nov. 8, 1795	James Markland to Betsy Kum
86	July 25, 1795	Blackstone Howard to Susannah Lee
87	Aug. 20, 1795	Allen Hill to Sally Garrett
88		John Smallwood to ____
89	Dec. 22, 1795	Samuel Hill to Fanny Moore
90	Nov. 4, 1795	Joseph Ore to Jenny Kelso
91	Nov. 4, 1795	Andrew Carson to Judith Nichols
92	June 23, 1795	George Henderson to Eleanor Campbell
93	Feb. 7, 1795	A. Still to Jenny Campbell
94	May 9, 1795	Robert Liggate to Florence Russel
95	May 5, 1795	James Gowan to Peggy Russell
96	Feb. 7, 1795	David Campbell to Nina Modrell
97	Feb. 2, 1795	Oliver Wallace to Thankful Harris
98	Jan. 18, 1795	Jno. Woodert to Rachel Williams
99	Dec. 4, 1795	Wm. Nelson to Molly Mickell
100	Dec. 19, 1796	Robert Kennedy (Kenney) to Mary Russell
101	Feb. 15, 1796	Jno. Henry to Susy McGlosthlin
102	Mar. 29, 1796	David Black to Mary Milles
103	Aug. 13, 1796	Wm. Patton to Mary W. Edgar
104	June 17, 1796	William Denton to Catherine Denton
105	May 6, 1796	James Gowan to Betsy Doherty
106	Aug. 22, 1796	Lion Bradley to Mary Wilson
107	Aug. 1, 1796	James Chilton to Nancy Clark
108	Aug. 2, 1796	Joseph Tipton to Lucy Potters
109	Aug. 6, 1976	Thos. Adamson to Rachel Williams
110	May 23, 1796	Robert Adams to Sally Eastridge
111	Feb. 23, 1796	Thomas Shadden to Peggy Aiken
112	Feb. 1, 1796	Philip Huff to Mina Turman
113	Feb. 4, 1796	Geo. McGihan to Margaret Sullivan
114	Feb. 21, 1796	Robert Berry to Susannah Simons
115	Feb. 22, 1796	Bartyelle Anderson to Mary Baker
116	Sept. 27, 1796	Geo. German to Abigail Williams
117	Feb. 24, 1796	John Webb to Rachael Ward
118	Oct. 8, 1796	Walter Kenedy to Anny Huzy
119	Nov. 5, 1796	David Day to Rosanna McDonald
120	Sept. 24, 1796	Joseph Sullins to Molly Hoskins
121	Sept. 30, 1796	Nathan Wright to Phebe ____
122	Aug. 12, 1796	Samuel McCuistion to Isabella Scott
123	Nov. 6, 1796	John Inman to Susannah Clark
124	Nov. 11, 1796	Samuel McCormack to Polly Cummins
125	Dec. 2, 1796	Zachariah Riddle to Polly Howard
126	Oct. 8, 1796	James Lyon to Nancy Hanney
127	Dec. 13, 1796	Jno. Hughs to Suzannah Hays
128	Dec. 13, 1796	Caleb Gannon to Jenny Walker
129	Dec. 2, 1796	Allen Thompson to ____
130	July 13, 1796	Seth Moore to Mary Ward
131	April 4, 1796	John Parks to Nancy Hoskins
132	Mar. 4, 1796	David Blackburn to Mary Miller

133	March 10, 1796	Wm. Leggett to Easter Hays
134	Nov. 10, 1796	David Moore to Peggy Foress
135	June 28, 1796	John Neilson to Sally McGee
136	Dec. 20, 1796	Wm. Doherty to Nancy Doherty
137	Aug. 3, 1796	Isaac Brazelton to Anny Johnston
138	Nov. 2, 1795	Isarel Mayfield to Polly Pruit
139	May 3, 1796	Wm. Johnson to Sally Forbias
140	Dec. 28, 1796	Jno. Campbell to Sarah Vance
141	May 4, 1796	Joseph Denton to Charity Bailey
142	Aug. 30, 1796	John Kirk to Nancy Samples
143	Feb. 1, 1796	Jno. Cartolon to Susannah Garrison
144	Oct. 20, 1795	Thomas Readsno o ____
145	Aug. 8, 1797	Thomas Mathes to Katherine Copeland
146	Aug. 9, 1797	James Cunningham to Katharine Keeger
147	May 24, 1797	Robert Lowery to Jean Denton
148	July 18, 1797	George Ray to Mary Blair
149	Jan. 15, 1797	Jacob Tarwater to Sarah Rolin
150	Jan. 18, 1797	Jesse Moore to Martha Rogers
151	July 18, 1808	Jno. Clinkinheard to Polly Carter
152	Oct. 15, 1797	Stephen Riddler to Sally Bell
153	May 4, 1797	C. Mannel to Delilah Brown
154	Nov. 21, 1797	James Caffee to Charity Murry
155	Oct. 20, 1797	Robert Snodgrass to Jenny Boyd
156	Jan. 31, 1797	Nicholas Copeland to Dorcas Mathes
157	Jan. 7, 1797	David Stephens to Rebecca McClannahan
158	Sept. 28, 1797	Reuben McFarland to Martha Campbell
159	Jan. 9, 1797	Henry Randolph to Susannah Myers
160	Sept. 26, 1797	Edward Pankee to Sally Myers
161	Feb. 9, 1797	Joseph Denson to Martha Gowan
162	Dec. 1, 1797	Robert Reed to S. Chapman
163	July 15, 1797	John Greenlee to Elizabeth Sutherland
164	April 25, 1797	Joseph Witt to L. Earls
165	March 4, 1797	Robert Turner to Leah M. David
166	June 12, 1797	Thomas Smith to Polly Brothers
167	May 24, 1797	Robert Lowery to Jean Denton
169		A. Booker to Keziah Huff
170	May 2, 1797	Patrick Burns to Janet King
171	March 13, 1797	James Hunter to Isabella Ritchey
172	Dec. 23, 1797	Wm. Jennings to Betsy Baker
173	July 20, 1797	John Morgan to Lucy Morgan
174	Sept. 5, 1797	John Hornback to Anna Forrest
175	March 26, 1797	John Myers to ____
176	May 1, 1797	L. Fine to E. Netherson
177	Oct. 15, 1797	Jno. Bell to Sally Irwin
178	July 1, 1797	Andrew Farmer to Elizabeth Parkey
179	April 15, 1797	James Hodges to Rebecca Church
180	Feb. 7, 1797	Jeffries Potter to Nancy Morgan

181	June 23, 1797	James Campbell to Elizabeth Smith
182	March 12, 1797	Charles Neal to Ruth Markman
183	May 5, 1797	Dudley Cox to Leanne Neal
184	March 15, 1797	William Love to Polly Inman
185	April 23, 1797	Bartley Renno to Sarah Driskell
186	Sept. 15, 1797	John Black to Sally Cooper
187	March 27, 1797	Samuel Bingham to Lucy Alexander
188	July 11, 1797	James Harrison to Liddie Bottoms
189	Aug. 5, 1797	James Hickman to Elizabeth Turner
190	June 15, 1797	Samuel Baker to Nancy Ford
191	July 18, 1797	David Moyers to Margaret Gray
192	Feb. 8, 1797	Samuel Lyle to Margara Haddy
193	Feb. 8, 1797	Samuel Haill to Ann Hampton
194	Feb. 8, 1797	Andrew McCuistion to _____ Rankin
195	Aug. 8, 1797	Robt. Dean to Polly Chapman
196	Aug. 4, 1797	Jno. Hickman to _____
197	June 18, 1898	Noah Ashley to Rachel Moore
198	June 14, 1797	L. Todd to Delia Edwards
199	March 31, 1797	Jno. Farban to (can't read name)
200	Feb. 6, 1797	Abner Frazer to Eliza Woodward
201	Nov. 9, 1797	John Roberts to Jennie Patton
202	Nov. 9, 1979	William Doherty to _____
203	Dec. 16, 1797	James Kirkpatrick to Polly Hill
204	Oct. 24, 1797	John Gwin to Mary Hanks
205	Oct. 14, 1797	John Frame to Elizabeth Frame
206	Nov. 14, 1797	Sampson Nation to _____
207	Nov. 14, 1797	Moses Balinger to Dorothy Turner
208	Oct. 29, 1797	Andrew Sutherland to Lidian Williams
209	Nov. 21, 1797	John Odle to Nancy Moore
210	Dec. 8, 1797	Jesse Roddye to Jennie Mchafy
211	Oct. 6, 1797	Henry Haggard to Lucy Randolph
212	Dec. 25, 1797	Isaac K. Elley to Agnes Keth
213	Jan. 3, 1797	Mathew Pheniz to Rosanna Sandusky
214	Jan. 20, 1797	Samuel White to Nancy Rankin
215	March 9, 1797	Paul McDonald to Dolly Outlaw
216	April 4, 1797	Henry Crewell to Sallie Copeland
217	Jan. 31, 1797	William Gibson to Margaret Johnston
218	Jan. 3, 1797	Vincent Larkins to Elizabeth Holmes
219	May 24, 1797	Peter Majors to Polly Wright
220	Feb. 6, 1797	Thomas Niel to Nancy Flippin
221	Dec. 26, 1797	Elijah Witt to Sarah Bottom
222	Jan. 15, 1797	Thomas Rogers to Mary Donelson
223	Feb. 6, 1797	William Bradshaw to Margaret Bingham
224	June 2, 1797	David Lewis to Elizabeth Bugler
225	Aug. 11, 1797	George Brindle to Martha Barclay
226	Aug. 14, 1798	Freeman Runnean to Patty Swainey
227	March 19, 1798	Robert Evans to Elizabeth Davidson
228	Nov. 6, 1798	Benjamine Prater to Nancy Lane
229	Oct. 3, 1798	James McFarland to Elizabeth Carmichael

230	July 23, 1798	Abner Majors to Rachel Roddye
231	Dec. 24, 1798	J. Hebbert to Olive Cox
232	June 13, 1798	Reuben George to Nancy Hodges
233	Dec. 27, 1798	Wm. David to Abialla Hargrave
234	Dec. 3, 1798	Edward Hampston to Jean Nully
235	Sept. 1798	John Reams to Betty Hanson
236	Nov. 12, 1798	John McLow to Peggy Kitccuel
237	Nov. 15, 1798	Abner Lowe to Rebecca West
238	Dec. 30, 1798	Dave Rowx to Sally Bows
239	_____ 1798	James Smelser to Elizabeth Johnson
240	Feb. 26, 1798	Charles Meek to Elizabeth Lambert
241	July 14, 1798	Wm. Inman to Elinor Wilson
242	July 15, 1798	Berry Bradford to Polly McFarland
243	April 9, 1798	John Petty to Nancy Evans
244	May 19, 1798	Wm. Neil to Hannah Jones
245	May 19, 1798	James Wright to Bridget Roddye
246	Sept. 4, 1798	Isaac Barton to _____
247	July 19, 1798	John Wilson to Ruth Moore
248	Feb. 29, 1798	Edward Stephenson to Elizabeth Campbell
249	April 16, 1798	John Rucker to Jean Carman
250	May 17, 1798	Philip Free to L. Ellis
251	April 19, 1798	James David to Nollie Wilson
252	May 21, 1798	Wm. Montgomery to Susannah McMeans
253	July 17, 1798	Wm. Baker to Polly Buller
254	July 24, 1798	Joel Cox to Margaret Wellhill
255	Jan. 10, 1798	Edward George and Polly Hambright
256	Feb. 1, 1798	John Giger and Susanah Creech
257	May 28, 1798	Valentine Molden to V. Robertson
258	May 15, 1798	James Bunn to Elizabeth Brittain
259	_____ 1798	Wm. Blackburn to Amy Samples
260	Oct. 11, 1798	Alex. McDonald to Hannah Kirkpatrick
261	June 30, 1798	Thomas Jones to Nancy Tucker
262	June 27, 1798	Wm. Goen to Betsy Jones
263	Aug. 12, 1798	Dudley Talley to Nancy Davis
264	June 27, 1798	David Jones to Mary Harrison
265	April 17, 1798	Nath. Gist to Nancy Copeland
266	_____ 1798	Wm. Cllahan to Rachel Vanhoun
267	March 9, 1798	Robert Johnson to D. Holmes
268	Feb. 15, 1798	James Guthrie to Isabelle Trotter
269	April 21, 1798	Jesse Lea to Elizabeth Failey
270	Jan. 15, 1798	Loyd Eddy to Margaret Biddle
271	July 18, 1798	Joseph Seabourne to Mary Wilhight
272	April 19, 1798	Francis Hickman to Leah Coffee
273	April 1, 1798	Wm. Love to Ellender Shelton.
274	Sept. 18, 1799	John Carson to Polly Carson
275	Nov. 11, 1799	Jacob Cofman to Nancy Walder
276	Jan. 9, 1799	Alex Howard to F. Wood
277	Feb. 21, 1799	John Magers to Keziah Duncan

JEFFERSON COUNTY MARRIAGES

278	_____ 1799	James Odle to Delilah Fox
279	Oct. 22, 1799	Thomas W. Frazier to Polly Sterling
280	Oct. 21, 1799	Jno. Cox to Sally Kelly
281	Jan. 22, 1799	Edward Springer to Katherine Keyler
282	Jan. 24, 1799	John Montgomery to Peggy Alexander
283	Aug. 24, 1799	Edward Armes to N. Mitchell
284	Dec. 15, 1799	Benjamine Goins to Anny Jones
285	Sept. 30, 1799	John Markison to Nancy Baker
286	Oct. 22, 1799	Wm. Mills to Sarah Maulsly
287	Oct. 20, 1799	Wm. Moore to Jean Hutner
288	June 11, 1799	Joseph Coons to Deborah Combs
289	Oct. 20, 1799	Wm. Dean to Aylse Woodward
290	Jan. 25, 1799	Henry Bradford to Rachael McFarland
291	July 15, 1798	John Denton to Polly Denton
292	Oct. 23, 1799	Samuel McSpadden to Nancy Harris
293	Oct. 22, 1799	John Seahorn Jr. to Polly Graham
294	Jan. 24, 1799	James M. Craig to Rebecca Russell
295	Jan. 22, 1799	John Rogers to Rachel Russell
296	Feb. 22, 1799	Owen Bresmet to Thirby Brown
297	Oct. 24, 1799	Joseph Williams to Sophia Thornburg
298	Jan. 24, 1799	Samuel George to Barbara Leeth
299	Jan. 1, 1799	Joel Watkins to Patsy Baker
300	Oct. 23, 1799	Jeremiah Riddle to Polly Majors
301	April 12, 1799	Thomas Wyatt to Polly Davis
302	March 17, 1799	John Carrady to Julitha Cox
303	Jan. 21, 1799	Zachariah Mills to Hannah Mendenhall
304	Oct. 24, 1799	John Green to Mary Sterling
305	Aug. 24, 1799	William Petty to Elizabeth Shelly
306	April 30, 1799	John McFarland to Betsy Davis
307	Jan. 4, 1799	Peter Cluck to Susan Solomon
308	Dec. 5, 1800	David Neil to Elizabeth McClanahan
309	Aug. 25, 1800	Abner Cannon to Mary Mackroberts
310	Jan. 22, 1800	Alexander Ritchey to Elizabeth Maxwell
311	May 8, 1800	Zachariah Cannon to Elizabeth Edgar
312	Dec. 5, 1800	Jacob Bowman to Rebecca Newman
313	Oct. 24, 1800	John Duncan to Jeannette McCullock
314	Nov. 15, 1800	John Petty to Elizabeth Britton
315	Nov. 26, 1800	John Williams to _____
316	Dec. 1, 1800	Parker Carradine to Lettice Thornton
317	Feb. 17, 1800	Isaah Coppock to Isabella Deneson
318	Jan. 2, 1800	Brittan Cross to Mary Parks
319	Jan. 22, 1800	George Leith to Elizabeth Arthur
320	Aug. 4, 1800	William Jennings to Polly Spangler

321	_____	Robert Anderson to _____
322	March 4, 1800	John N. Been (Been) to Jean McFarland
323	Jan. 20, 1800	William Pope to Margaret Maples
324	Oct. 24, 1800	William Shadden to Elizabeth Hayes
325	Dec. 9, 1800	William Stewart to Rebecca Pratt
326	Jan. 7, 1800	Alexander Howard to Elizabeth Wood
327	Jan. 26, 1800	William Crump to Phebe Crows
328	July 18, 1800	Ezekiel Greseum to Elinor Walker
329	Feb. 18, 1800	John Kinkade to Elizabeth Maloney
330	Aug. 25, 1800	George Nickles to Elizabeth Niel
331	Feb. 24, 1800	William Jones to Mary Howard
332	Nov. 29, 1800	John Ballinger to Sarah Small
333	Aug. 23, 1800	Lewes Taylor to Elizabeth _____
334	March 18, 1800	Isaac Wilson to Nancy Morris
335	Jan. 22, 1800	David Jones to Ann Morris
336	April 22, 1800	Joseph Newman to Catherine Cate
337	Not dated	Jeremiah Nicholson to Rebecca McQucan
338	Aug. 18, 1800	John Grisham to Peggy Barnes
339	Dec. 13, 1800	David Wilson to Hannah Retta Inman
340	July 22, 1800	Andrew Gowan to Mary Reneau
341	April 20, 1800	James Davidson to Jenny Bant (or Beny)
342	April 22, 1800	James Bradshaw to Susannah Massey
343	Jan. 23, 1800	James Russel to Elizabeth Hammond
344	April 22, 1800	Littleton Williams to Sarah Barker
345	April 22, 1800	John Malcom to Anne Montgomery
346	May 31, 1800	John Ray to Huddy Ellis
347	Aug. 18, 1800	John Kimbro to Susannah Gressum
348	Aug. 8, 1800	John Hargrave to Hannah Hamson
349	Aug. 18, 1800	Thomas Drunen to Elizabeth Day
350	June 2, 1800	Jesse Cobbtto to Jenny Driskill
351	Jan. 22, 1800	Edward Nation to Deborah Hawkins
352	July 13, 1800	David Snodgrass to Nancy Carson
353	July 20, 1800	B. Poindexter and Rachel Patton
354	Oct. 25, 1800	John Gavins to Charlotte Campbell
355	July 23, 1800	David Morrow to Celiah Doherty
356	Oct. 24, 1800	Wm. Malcom to Nancy Shadden
357	July 22, 1800	James Barnes to Elizabeth Julias
358	Oct. 8, 1800	George Blackburn to Patsy Neeley
359	July 21, 1800	Joseph Mills to Rebecca Stilwell
360	Aug. 6, 1801	Thomas Little to Mary Houston
361	Feb. 21, 1801	Francis Clark to Polly Shelton
362	April 22, 1801	Alexander Cannon to Dice Duncan
363	Jan. 31, 1801	James McCarrol to Ester Routh
364	March 13, 1801	John Smith to Elizabeth Pugmoor (Prigmore)

365	July 8, 1801	Thomas Davis to Sarah Hill
366	July 25, 1801	Wm. Hodges to Elizabeth Milles
367	Oct. 14, 1801	Wm. Dameon to Sarah Roddye
368	Aug. 21, 1801	Wilke Kirkpatrick to Sarah Hoskins
369	Oct. 22, 1801	John Cisco to Betsy Morris
370	Dec. 20, 1801	Jacob Sehorn to Nancy Galbraith
371	Jan. 20, 1801	Wm. Baker to Hannah Edwards
372	March 19, 1801	James McDonald to Sallie Mays
373	Aug. 31, 1801	Jacob Lake to Susannah Williams
374	July 22, 1801	Thomas Williams to Rachel Longacre
375	July 25, 1801	Stephen Mundenhall to Nancy Gann
376	July 21, 1801	John Love to Nancy McSpadden
377	July 20, 1801	Thomas Calahan to Rachel Daniel
378	Sept. 29, 1801	Thomas Horton to Elizabeth Eleax
379	Sept. 19, 1801	Garritt Lane to Nancy Hall
380	July 20, 1801	Michael Montgomery to Martha County
381	Dec. 4, 1801	R. Shumate to Elizabeth
382	June 1, 1801	William Conway to Mary Evans
383	July 21, 1801	John Renno to Cisse Renno
384	Jan. 19, 1801	John Layman to Nancy McGuire
385	March 4, 1801	Major Lee to Rhoda Jarnagin
386	March 23, 1801	James Davis to Agnes Barker
387	Sept. 26, 1801	Thomas Balinger to Sallie Stafford
388	Feb. 20, 1801	Alexander Thompson to Hannah Donelson
389	April 20, 1801	George Rains to Susannah Jones
390	June 22, 1801	Robert Dyer to Sallie Cheek
391	June 8, 1801	William Jack to Esther
392	June 4, 1801	Thomas Green to Catherine Horner
393	May 22, 1801	Jonathan Hill to Mary Miller
394	Sept. 21, 1801	Caliborne Brown to Ann W. Lovey
395	April 21, 1801	Frederick Saunders to Patsey Jones
396	July 20, 1801	David Layman to Nancy Ebbs
397	July 29, 1802	Wm. Harrison to Nancy Adams
398	July 29, 1802	Phillip Sevier to Mary Bevely
399	Feb. 16, 1802	Isham Adams to Fanny McClannahan
400	Jan. 29, 1802	Phillip Sevier to Mary Bevely
401	Nov. 1, 1802	Nicholason Peach to Nancy Henderson
402	Dec. 20, 1802	Morgan Thornburgh to Hannah Harle
403	Dec. 6, 1802	Stephen Day to Barbara Weaver
404	Sept. 29, 1802	Conrad Easterly to Elizabeth
405	Sept. 18, 1802	John Colplant to Susan Honore
406	Sept. 4, 1802	George Cassell to Elizabeth Davis
407	Oct. 10, 1802	Benjamine DeWitt to Susannah Weaver
408	June 22, 1802	Jeremiah Inman to Prudence Battom

409	June 3, 1802	John Snodgrass to Rhoda Mazr (Marr)
410	Oct. 15, 1802	Elias Majors to Margaret Floyd
411	July 15, 1802	Samuel McPherson to Betsy Campbell
412	April 29, 1802	Andrew Blackburn to Catherine McGuire
413	July 3, 1802	Jacob Clark to Eda Solimon
414	July 5, 1802	Joel Thornburgh to Dianna Perdy
415	Jan. 18, 1802	Isaac Williams to Millie Gobson (Dodson)
416	Sept. 22, 1802	Jno. Blackburn to Elizabeth McGirt
417	Dec. 21, 1802	George Larew to Cithia Chilton
418	July 28, 1802	Lewis Larver to H. Felps
419	July 29, 1802	Tilman Hurley to Polly Teney
420	July 20, 1802	Moses Templar to Barbara Inman
421	Dec. 24, 1802	Josiah Denton to Catherine Seahorn
422	Feb. 23, 1802	Edmund Hodges to Rachel Lennon
423	May 19, 1802	Henry Clock to Hannah Longacre
424	May 26, 1802	David Lowery to Levice Seahorn
425	Jan. 1, 1802	James Raulstone to Jennie Syms
426	Jan. 1, 1802	William Burriss to Elizabeth Baily
427	April 19, 1802	William Salvage to Judith Tucker
428	May 4, 1802	James Bradford to Catherine W. Keith
429	March 3, 1802	Thomas McSpadden to Abagail
430	Jan. 19, 1802	William Wilson to Polly Henderson
431	Feb. 16, 1802	Robert Elder to S. Moore
432	Oct. 21,	Lewes Russell to Esther Horner
433	Oct. 17, 1802	John Backholder to Elizabeth Cate
434	June 15, 1802	William Parker to Patsy Jackson
435	Nov. 8, 1802	James Carmichael to Elizabeth Barton
436	July 20, 1802	William Juban (Julian) to Nancy Whitlock
437	Dec. 8, 1802	Samuel Saffield to Betsy Cox
438	May 29, 1802	Hamilton Bradford to Jennie Hill
439	April 23, 1802	Hamilton Bradford to Polly Doherty
440	Feb. 13, 1802	Thomas Chilton to Susannah Inman
441	April 6, 1802	George Rowland to Isabella Patton
442	June 15, 1802	Enos Johnson to Rhoda Tanner
443	April 8, 1802?	William Merret to Ann Pendill
444	April 14, 1802	Peter Exkle to Catherine Swingle
445	Jan. 1, 1802	Samuel Raulstone to Betsey Lowery
446	April 20, 1802	Jared Newman to Margaret Campbell
447	April 20, 1802	Thomas Cate to Ane Wilhite
448	April 19, 1802	Edward Stephens to Rebecca Penn
449	April 20, 1802	Charles McGuire to Sally Doherty

450	Jan. 19, 1802	James Lewes to Rebecca Lowery
451	March 17, 1802	Samuel Todd to Ann Harrison
452	May 29, 1802	John Briggs to Phoebe Good
453	March 3, 1802	Ezekiel Williams to Polly McDonald
454	Oct. 19, 1802	Moses Raulstone to Polly Denny
455	Dec. 4, 1803	David Beck to Sarah Hunter
456	Dec. 4, 1803	Jonathan Keney to Polly McClanghlind
457	April 20, 1803	Jacob Bear to Sarah Taylor
458	Feb. 29, 1803	Wm. Riggs to Millie McGhee
459	Feb. 3, 1803	Wm. Crockett and Rebecca Elliott
460	May 23, 1803	James Hodges to Sally Deammerl
461	Feb. 3, 1804	Michael Woods to Agnes Gililland
462	May 23, 1803	Aaron Williams and Charity Nation
463	April 21, 1803	Thomas Hammond to Polly Neely
464	Jan. 3, 1803	Joseph Cross to Polly Hoskins
465	Jan. 13, 1803	James Hoskins to Isabella Galbraith
466	Feb. 17, 1803	Jesse Doggett to Jenny Claxton
467	Jan. 17, 1803	Wm. Clinkerbird to Asspitis Harp
468	Dec. 27, 1803	Abraham Sutherland to Martha Curvinling
469	July 18, 1803	John Miller to Patty Moore
470	Oct. 17, 1803	Robert D. Eaton to Janny Clambilain (Chamberlain)
471	Jan. 20, 1803	Peter Trammon to Tabitha Bowax
472	July 19, 1803	Joseph McDonald to Patty Bryan
473	July 18, 1803	Richardson Davidson to Catherine Mills
474	July 19, 1803	Wm. Hickman to _____ Wilhoit
475	Sept. 27, 1803	John Pickens to Patsy Jarnagin
476	Aug. 6, 1803	Thomas Crosly to Polly Horner
477	Nov. 9, 1803	John Carson to Florence Haggard
478	Aug. 2, 1803	Turman Shelton to Rachel Inman
479	Aug. 20, 1803	Joseph Coppock to Lucy Bingham
480	Aug. 23, 1803	Benjamine Ketching to Elizabeth Witt
481	Nov. 2, 1803	Henry Merrick to Susannah Robinson
482	April 12, 1803	Wm. Routh to Pheba Hodges
483	Aug. 30, 1803	Samuel Bradshaw to Darkie Pegmore (Prigmore)
484	Oct. 31, 1803	John Jack to Ann Neeley
485	Sept. 12, 1803	George Cluck to Betsy Sutherland
486	April 18, 1803	Wm. Patton to Sally Bidwell
487	Jan. 25, 1803	Thomas Doke to Elizabeth Hope
488	Jan. 26, 1803	Thomas Walker to Mary Cluck
489	Dec. 21, 1803	Samuel Carson to Annie Jarnagin
490	Aug. 31, 1803	Gabriel Keeth to Tabitha Roran
491	March 1, 1803	John Meels to Sallie Coffman
492	March 1, 1803	Amos Thornbrough to Levinia Tucker
493	April 21, 1803	William Golden to Sarah Haworth

494	Feb. 26, 1803	Benjamine Crump to Susannah Doggett
495	Sept. 7, 1803	Thomas White to Jennie Hale
496	June 20, 1803	William Mendenhall to Elizabeth Carper
497	Jan. 4, 1802/3	Reuben Angle to Betsey Hodges
498	Oct. 18, 1803	Alexander Caldwell and Catherine Aiken
499	Nov. 26, 1803	Methew Perrine to Betsey Longacre
500	Oct. 1, 1803	Richard Thornbrough to Elinor Molsby
501	April 6, 1803	John Williams to Patsy Cox
502	Jan. 18, 1803	William Brazelton to Elizabeth Deans
503	Oct. 17, 1803	Ferrell Hester to Elinor McGhee
504	July 18, 1803	William Elder to Rebecca Cates
505	Dec. 24, 1803	Thomas Griffin to Polly Hill
506	Nov. 12, 1803	John Rorex to Deliah Campbell
507	Nov. 26, 1803	Andrew Langacre to Ann Longacre
508	Dec. 29, 1803	Jacob Miller to Elizabeth Preddy
509	Oct. 16, 1803	David Vance to R. Taylor
510	Dec. 17, 1804	Jacob Wilson to Jennie Brooks
511	Nov. 22, 1804	Thomas Williams to Patty Cheek
512	Jan. 14, 1804	Henry Wilkes to Elizabeth Inman (could be Walker instead of Wilkes)
513	Dec. 3, 1804	Henry Brown to Sarah Sutherland
514	Sept. 21, 1804	Jerry Hains to Nancy Sheek
515	April 16, 1804	Andrew Sinely to Rebeccah Deaton
516	Sept. 11, 1804	Moses Ballinger to Nancy Bird
517	Jan. 19, 1804	John Jacob to Mary alias Polly Taylor
518	Nov. 14, 1804	Wm. Hodges to Centy Webb
519	Nov. 15, 1804	Thomas Hawkins to Susannah Culp
520	Nov. 22, 1804	Isaac Canhooser to Agnes Baker
521	Oct. 16, 1804	Isaac Copper to Abigail Thornbrough
522	Oct. 29, 1804	Daniel Davis to Lenny Larson
523	Nov. 14, 1804	John Cooper to Mary Hammond
524	Jan. 20, 1804	L. Adams to Elizabeth Pernonat
525	Oct. 16, 1804	John Vanhooser to Nancy Daniel
526	Oct. 21, 1804	David Crockett to Margaret Elder
527	Nov. 13, 1804	Robert Gentry to Rachael West
528	Sept. 18, 1804	Richard Webb to Nancy Brooks
529	Oct. 22, 1804	Joseph Ellis to J. Gorrmen
530	Oct. 31, 1805	Thomas Cannon to Sallie Bettis
531	Oct. 16, 1804	Wm. Peacock to Susannah Roach
532	Dec. 30, 1804	George Hoskins to Jennina Parks
533	Nov. 28, 1804	Joseph Mooney to Nancy Blanner
534	Oct. 16, 1804	Simon York to Ann Wood
535	Jan. 7, 1804	Chas. B. Kelso to Elizabeth Campbell
536	Dec. 20, 1804	Jas. Dodson to Lucy Danis
537	Dec. 21, 1804	Samuel Newman to Sallie Lennox

538	April 4, 1804	Wm. Ellis to Polly Elliott
539	May 29, 1804	Thomas Bales to Marty Bone
540		James Axen to _____
541	March 28, 1804	Robert Stephenson to Rebecca Newman
542	March 23, 1804	Richard Gorshan to Polly Barnes
543	July 10, 1804	Martin Jones to Rhoda Hodges
544	July 28, 1804	Jesse Hill to Elizabeth Blackburn
546	Aug. 13, 1804	David Williams to Rutha Beaker
547	Sept. 5, 1804	Edward Blackburn to Margaret McGirt
548	May 25, 1804	Wm. Jones to Elizabeth Randolph
549	Oct. 2, 1804	James Blackstone to Polly Shelly
550	July 30, 1804	Nathaniel Witt to Mary Cate
551	June 3, 1804	George Gigor to Betha Henderson
552	Sept. 4, 1804	Joseph Brittain to Sally Cheek
553	Oct. 4, 1804	Joseph Copeland to Rebecca McMean
554	April 2, 1804	Furgerson Jackson to Permelia West
555	Oct. 11, 1804	Stephen Dyer to Elizabeth Dameron
556	March 27, 1804	James McSpadden to Ealsey Galbreath
557	Feb. 8, 1804	Abraham Meger to Joycey Ford
558	Jan. 16, 1804	Absolom Mendenhall to Judith Labeapeco
559	Aug. 10, 1804	John Crow to Nancy Wilson
560	Jan. 29, 1804	Wm. West to Peggy Inman
561	July 17, 1804	Robert Patton to W. Thornbrough
562	July 17, 1804	Jas. Hornback to Sarah Dean
563	Sept. 10, 1804	Samuel Lowery to Mary Spangler
564	Aug. 30, 1804	Samuel Jones to Pheba Howard
565	July 31, 1804	Jesse Ellis to Jane Elliott
566	May 10, 1804	James King to Nancy Parks
567	April 17, 1804	Wm. Mauldby to Mary Cox
568	June 20, 1804	Alexander McClannahan to Lemal Taylor
569	June 27, 1804	Wm. Hembrick to Eleanor Ford
570	May 16, 1804	Wm. McClannahan to Sallie Cos
571	Feb. 18, 1805	Andrew Gannon to Anne White
572	July 16, 1804	Richard Thornburgh to Margaret Chase
573	Aug. 15, 1804	Amos Ashmore to Patience Mackguire
574	June 19, 1804	John Carson to Nancy Blackburn
575	April 6, 1804	George Jack to Polly Doherty
576	Sept. 17, 1805	Richard Graves to Casandra Riggs
577	Sept. 21, 1805	Thomas Ellis to Sarah Lowery
578	Sept. 7, 1805	Alexander McKaney to Susannah Thompson
579	Oct. 21, 1805	Wiley Tucker to Rebecca Privett
580	Sept. 10, 1805	Joseph Nicholson to Annie McGuire
581	Aug. 3, 1805	James Howel to Nancy Davis
582	April 27, 1805	Reed Cox to Mary Carper
583	Oct. 11, 1805	James Bates to Charity Havard

13

584	Nov. 2, 1805	Jarvis Capman to Jemina Turner
585	Oct. 22, 1805	Levi Day to Malinda Smith
586	Nov. 25, 1805	Garrett Reese to Betsey _____
587	July 11, 1805	Isaiah Hurley to Anna Holdway
588	June 15, 1805	A. Taylor to Jenny Inman
589	April 16, 1805	Wm. Whaley to Elizabeth Lracy (Lacy)
590	April 27, 1805	John Gurry to Elizabeth Elliott
591	March 26, 1805	John Collins to Mahaley Sehorn
592	Sept. 7, 1805	Wm. McCann to Sally Hill
593	Aug. 31, 1805	Robert McFarland to Mary Cox
594	Oct. 20, 1805	Robert McClannahan to Fanny Moore
595	March 8, 1805	Alexander Hays to Peggy Sheddan
596	March 20, 1805	Douglass Puckett to Jennet Meals
597	March 8, 1805	Joseph Sheddan to Rachel Hays
598	Jan. 21, 1805	Wm. Hains to Betsy Cocke
599	Sept. 27, 1805	John McClannahan to Betsy Simpson
600	Sept. 27, 1805	Isaac McMean to Drucilla Allen
601	Aug. 22, 1805	John Moore to Polly Priddy
602	Oct. 8, 1805	John Lea to Anna Roddy
603	Oct. 12, 1805	Peter Tackett to Rebecca Coontz
604	May 21, 1805	James Helton to Keziah Cortley
605	May 21, 1805	Wm. Cofman to Sally White
606	May 21, 1805	Richard Driner to Mary Day
607	Feb. 26, 1805	David Elmore to Elizabeth Hammon
608	Sept. 28, 1805	Richard Lewis to Elizabeth Manley
609	July 16, 1805	Robert McCuistian to Isabella Rankin
610	April 20, 1805	Morgan Williams to Nancy Royal
611	Dec. 28, 1805	Ezekiel Inman to Mathilda Taylor
612	Oct. 22, 1805	John Hays to Polly Shadden
613	Feb. 21, 1805	Reuben Mills to Nancy Lea
614	Jan. 8, 1805	James Blackburn to Catherine Jamison
615	July 2, 1805	John White to Polly Hanes
616	Feb. 3, 1805	Robert Howard to Patsey Blackburn
617	Feb. 5, 1805	Geo. W. Woods to Margery Snodgrass
618	Jan. 23, 1805	Jacob Slover to Martha Moore
619	Feb. 20, 1806	Samuel Ramsey and Betsy Beaver
620	Dec. 15, 1805	Champ Shirley to Polly Jackson
621	Feb. 4, 1806	John Ellis to Peggy Lowery
622	Feb. 19, 1806	Antepas Thomas to Nancy Riggs
623	March 1, 1806	Wm. Tate to Elizabeth Sheddan
624	July 10, 1806	John Cantling to Sally Moore
625	Oct. 14, 1806	John Engert to Polly Cate
626	June 4, 1806	Jonathan Carr to Elizabeth Wood
627	July 23, 1806	Job Self to Mary Goin
628	Oct. 20, 1806	John Douglass to Mary Camrelle
629	Oct. 6, 1806	John Routh to Jane Moore
630	Aug. 27, 1806	John Doss to Polly Danvman
631	July 22, 1806	William Perrian to Levica King
632	Sept. 5, 1806	John Williams to Sallie Hodgen
633	Aug. 26, 1806	John Smith to Leah Canley

14

634	Sept. 24, 1806	Christopher Bradshaw to Polly Davis
635	Sept. 24, 1806	Frederick Barnett to Elizabeth Davis
636	July 20, 1806	John Neely to Sallie Moore
637	July 13, 1806	Eli Witt to Nancy McNeely
638	July 2, 1806	Robert Hill to Betsy McFarland
639	Aug. 9, 1806	Archibald Campbell to Jenny Peck
640	July 2, 1806	Enos Johnson to Vina Helton
641	Aug. 23, 1806	Richard Grisham to Elizabeth Burns
642	April 22, 1806	James Harris to Jennie McSpadden
643	May 22, 1806	Hezekiah Brown to Ruth Casteel
644	May 13, 1806	William King to Patsy Blackstone
645	Oct. 25, 1806	William Smith to Nancy Nance
646	Oct. 25, 1806	Love Slaton to Peggy Staples
647	April 21, 1806	John Pate to Elizabeth Renno
648	April 11, 1806	William McBroom to Elizabeth Snodgrass
649	March 17, 1806	Thomas Snoddy to Jennie Blackburn
650	June 3, 1806	Green Williams to Ruth Givens
651	Nov. 2, 1806	John Copeland to Polly Hood
652	Dec. 15, 1806	B. Jarnagin to Susannah Lee
653	Feb. 16, 1806	Charles Stropea to D. Skeen
654	Aug. 30, 1806	Green Hambrick to Betsy Dameron
655	March 28, 1806	Adam Lowery to Peggy Doss
656	Oct. 25, 1806	Eli Hornback to Sallie Combs
657	June 14, 1806	William George to Lucy McFarland
658	July 4, 1806	B. Kimbrough to Rebecca Daniel
659	July 25, 1806	Leonard Sparks to Patsy Beard
660	Nov. 23, 1806	Nero Campbell to Nancy Bird
661	June 7, 1806	Thomas Dyer to Rachel Merrick
662	Jan. 3, 1806	Nicholas Yeager to Polly Robinson
663	July 15, 1806	William Bottom to Annie Witt
664	Oct. 2, 1806	Lancy Funderback to Hannah Pope
665	Oct. 21, 1806	Isaac Slover to Polly Layman
666	Dec. 26, 1806	Isaac Adams to Jerusha West
667	May 19, 1806	Hugh Martin to Sallie Russell
668	Jan. 22, 1806	Lemmel Mabee to Sarah Meek
669	Aug. 7, 1806	James McCuistain to Linea Bradshaw
670	March 22, 1806	Thomas Williams to B. Russell
671	May 12, 1806	Asa McGhee to Nancy Majors
672	June 18, 1806	Robert Ramsey to F. Beavers
673	Aug. 10, 1806	George Doherty to Polly Mathes
674	April 17, 1806	John Allen Swiniey to Sallie Swiniey
675	Jan. 2, 1806	John Dameron to Celia Hembrick
676	Jan. 20, 1806	Robert Canaday to Annie Turner
677	Nov. 3, 1806	Thomas Berry to Hannah Day
678	Sept. 20, 1806	James Walker to Catherine Cluck
679	April 8, 1806	John Carson to Ester Willer
680	Dec. 9, 1806	John Hill to Peggy Dobbin
681	March 14, 1806	Aaron Gibson to Jane Hornback

682	March 6; 1806	Uniah Johnson to Nancy Mitchell
683	Dec. 7, 1806	Francis Fonny to Mary Baker
684	Aug. 29, 1807	John Huffman to Martha Allen
685	Dec. 9, 1807	Phillip Sutherland to Charity Gibson
686	Sept. 30, 1807	Jesse Moore to Rebecca Stedman
687	March 24, 1807	Isaac Cate to Susannah Manard
688	Oct. 19, 1807	Jacob Vanhooser to Margare McGrennigel
689	Dec. 4, 1807	Caleb Pierce to Jane Frazier
690	April 20, 1807	Isaac Ruth to Sally Sloat
691	Feb. 5, 1807	Thomas Balkin to Delilah Vanhooser
692	Oct. 24, 1807	Thomas Jackson to Polly Cox
693	Dec. 14, 1807	John Harrison to Susannah Jackson
694	May 23, 1807	Lewis Lynn to Mina Beline
696	Sept. 9, 1807	Miller Doggett to Dillie Griffin
697	Nov. 21, 1807	Benj. Peck to Polly Henderson
698	Oct. 14, 1807	James Wood to Polly Renno
699	May 14, 1807	Richard Hicks to Polly Sampson
700	April 21, 1807	Nehemnah Day to Susannah Sutherland
701	Jan. 23, 1807	John Garritson to Annie Stephen
702	June 8, 1807	Henry Etter to Elizabeth Parks
703	June 3, 1807	John Mitchell to Ruth Henderson
704	July 23, 1807	John Ebbs to Mary Gingny
705	Feb. 10, 1807	P. Wilkerson to Jenny Seahorn
706	Sept. 4, 1807	Andrew Eaton to Elizabeth Churchman
707	Aug. 29, 1807	Joseph Lively to Rachel Taylor
708	May 4, 1807	Joseph McClannahan to Jane Snodgrass
709	Feb. 10, 1807	Samuel House to Mary Witt
710	May 1, 1807	Wm. Vance to Elizabeth Campbell
711	Jan. 21, 1807	James Neeley to Betsy Robinson
712	Dec. 28, 1807	John Claxey to Polly Brazell
713	Nov. 4, 1807	James Drake to Rosannah Neeley
714		Silas Hall to Elizabeth Moyers
715	Dec. 23, 1807	H. Witt to Mirian Skeen
716	April 21, 1807	Ebenezer Leith to Patsy Sellers
717	Aug. 18, 1807	David Ayes to Susannah Carmichael
718	Dec. 11, 1807	John Dellis to Anne Cumy
719	March 10, 1807	Joseph Hill to Susannah McMeen
720	March 27, 1807	Wm. Fine to Catherine Lively
721	Jan. 14, 1807	Benj. Brittain to Sarah Mathews
722	Jan. 23, 1807	James Hodges to Mary Barton
723	Aug. 9, 1807	A. Brown to Catharine Britain
724	April 29, 1807	Wm. White to Peggy Wilson
725	Aug. 7, 1807	Wm. Hickey to Ruth Longacre
726	Oct. 16, 1807	Valentine Gibson to Eliza Frazer
727	Oct. 16, 1807	Jesse Dunn to Nancy Twinney
728	July 22, 1807	John R. Inman to Jane Walker
729	July 23, 1807	James Wright to Sally Prewitt
730	Jan. 17, 1807	Robert Reed to Fanny James

731	April 21, 1807	Smith Merchant to Annie Mankins
732	Feb. 12, 1807	John Hill to Priscilla Hanes
733	July 18, 1807	Joseph Clemons to Tamps Jones
734	March 23, 1807	John West to Susannah Jackson
735	Dec. 4, 1807	John Henderson to Tabitha Keith
736	Feb. 13, 1807	George Cluck to Christiana Strupes
737	Dec. 11, 1807	Levi Lewis to Rebecca Spangler
738	March 16, 1807	William Neil to Sarah Davis
739	April 21, 1807	Thos. Hankins to Rebecca Hill
740	April 18, 1807	William Rennels to Sarah Barton
741	Jan. 28, 1807	Noah Haggard to Sallie Randolph
742	May 18, 1807	Peter Taafe to Mary Jinens
743	Feb. 28, 1807	William Treviathan to Barbara Warmon
744	Nov. 25, 1807	John Gannon to Sallie Elliott
745	Jan. 7, 1807	Thos. McSpadden to Elizabeth Walker
746	Feb. 4, 1807	George Long to Sarah Ford
747	June 18, 1807	John Gann to Sallie Edwards
748	June 24, 1807	Isaac Kimbro to Mary Randolph
749	Nov. 17, 1807	John Mays to Sallie Murray
750	June 15, 1807	Joseph Roper to Mary Henderson
751	Feb. 20, 1807	William Majors to Rachel McGhee
752	March 13, 1807	James Harrison to Hannah Lanstone
753	Sept. 30, 1808	S. Mills to Charity Thornburgh
754	Dec. 26, 1808	Caleb Hickman to Rebecca Hickman
755	Aug. 9, 1808	Goodwin Killen to Jane Sharp
756	July 22, 1808	John Brown to Elizabeth Hobert
757	June 16, 1808	Wm. Luck to M. Mills
758	April 19, 1808	James King to Peggy Ritchey
759	April 25, 1808	Christopher Merrian to Elender Sutherland
760	April 2, 1808	John Elder to Nancy Sullens
761	Feb. ___ 1808	John Nelson to Betsey Mansfield
762	Nov. 21, 1808	John H. Moore and Elizabeth Herman
763	Nov. 4, 1808	Jonathan Macy to Hannah Pierce
764	Oct. 17, 1808	William Hall to Tenna Sutherland
765	Oct. 24, 1808	M. Hall to Jane Thomas
766	Aug. 23, 1808	John Kimbrough to Rebecca Branson
767	Oct. 25, 1808	Joseph Combs to Nancy Woodall
768	May 6, 1808	L. Middleton to Jane Smith
769	July 15, 1808	Benj. D. Armstrong to Jenny Harrison
770	Sept. 12, 1808	John Ogle to Jenny Donaldson
771	Feb. 15, 1808	Henry Whitehurst to Leah Hide
772	Sept. 20, 1808	Charles Brooks to Jane Harris
773	July 20, 1808	Archibald Cordes to Elizabeth Robertson
774	July 16, 1808	Jeremiah Neal to Mary Thornburgh
775	July 18, 1808	John Clinkenbear to Polly Carter
776	May 16, 1808	Greenberry Taylor to Elizabeth Henes (Hanes)
777	Jan. 27, 1808	Christopher Hanes to Jane Grant
778	Jan. 29, 1808	David Kimbrough to Nancy Murphy

779	Feb. 22, 1808	Joseph Given to Millie Blackburn
780	Jan. 26, 1808	John Buckner to Polly Harrison
781	March 5, 1808	Elliott Peck to Nancy Campbell
782	April 13, 1808	John Brabson to Elizabeth Davis
783	April 10, 1808	Wm. Britain to Sarah Reed
784	Feb. 24, 1808	Wm. Legg to N. Coffman
785	June 27, 1808	Jno. E. Taylor to Sally White
786	Sept. 10, 1808	John Brannum to Judith Smith
787	Jan. 10, 1808	Jesse Hammer to Rebecca Blackburn
788	Jan. 2, 1808	Wm. Bell to Buley Johnson
789		Adam Carter to Winny Gates
790	Feb. 9, 1808	John Moffett to Eleanor Scott
791	April 19, 1808	Abraham Comes (Jones) to Sally Huggins
792	April 19, 1808	Eli Hankins to Nancy Smith
793	Dec. 7, 1808	Thomas Henderson to Mary Cowan
794	Dec. 17, 1808	Aaron Cornelins to Eleanor Fortner
795	Jan. 21, 1808	Alexr. Rodgers to Polly Simmons
796	June 25, 1800 (1808)	Jacob Brazelton to Margaret Carper
797	July 23, 1808	James Smith to Nice Middleton
798	Sept. 24, 1808	Elihu Milliken to Nancy Husk
799	Jan. 12, 1808	Charles Cobb to Sally Crawford
800	Nov. 29, 1808	Elijah Baker to Susannah Williams
801	Jan. 14, 1808	Nathaniel Day to Ruth Brittain
802	Aug. 3, 1808	Cleven Slatton to Sally Hickman
803	Jan. 7, 1808	John Baker to Elizabeth Ricketts
804	Oct. 12, 1808	George Sewell to Susannah Copeland
805	Sept. 2, 1808	Thomas Patterson to B. McDowell
806	Sept. 5, 1808	Moses Hammond to Dorcas Lay
807	Oct. 25, 1808	William Murphy to Elizabeth McDowell
808	Oct. 25, 1808	William Mathes to Rachel Balch
809	March 22, 1808	Robert Malcom to Jane Jones
810	May 13, 1808	Jesse Evans to Lavina Tipton
811	April 30, 1808	Jacob Aley to Susannah Bear
812	April 7, 1808	Strange Colthrop to Lavina Horner
813	Feb. 20, 1808	Joshua Massey to Elizabeth Ellis
814	May 20, 1808	Edward Templeton to Sarah Howard
815	Dec. 27, 1808	John Harrison to Peggy Parks
816	Dec. 7, 1808	John Peton to Margaret Cannon
817	Feb. 15, 1808	William Turner to Betsy Lathers
818	April 15, 1809	Isarel Willis to Patsy Adamson
819	Sept. 16, 1809	Reuben Churchman to Sarah Garner
820	May 24, 1809	William Houston to Grace McNight
821	Jan. 7, 1809	Thomas Hickman to Polly Hickman
822	Oct. 3, 1809	George Freshour to Pricilla Williams
823	Dec. 22, 1809	Robert Kelly to Malinda Moore
824	Oct. 21, 1809	Thomas Givens to Sophia Walker
825	Sept. 12, 1809	Jonathan Milles (Miller) to Annie Gibson

826	Sept. 28, 1809	Casper Branner to Maria Davis
827	Feb. 13, 1809	Thomas Mills to Mary Gibbons
828	Oct. 12, 1809	William Gibbons to Rebecca Carl
829	Jan. 8, 1809	John Reed to Lucretia Kelly
830	May 18, 1809	Hugh Cantrell to Susannah Simmonds
831	June 22, 1809	Alexr Hammil to Mary Ann Hodgan
832	Dec. 25, 1809	Benj. Longacre to Judah Perkins
833	March 22, 1809	Bradley Bettis to Francis Walker
834	Jan. 28, 1809	Jno. Ramsey to Ann Britain
835	Aug. 4, 1809	Richard Bradshaw to Lydia Pugmore (Prigmore)
836	Nov. 29, 1809	Adam Cantrell and Sarah Simmonds
837	April 9, 1809	James Prewitt to Sarah Inman
838	Jan. 31, 1809	Valentine Gibson to Catherine Harold
839	May 29, 1809	John Miller to Rhoda Patan (Patten)
840	Nov. 17, 1809	Phillip Rinehart to Lucrellia Ellis
841	Oct. 15, 1809	Joshua Clevenger to Elizabeth Janeway
842	April 13, 1809	Abel Gibson to Selah Harrold
843	June 1, 1809	John McSpadden to Nancy P. Carter
844	May 29, 1809	John Chilton to C. Clark
845	Feb. 18, 1809	John Shannon to Rachel Hickey
846	Oct. 28, 1809	Joseph Cox to Mary Line
847	Oct. 25, 1809	Leroy Taylor to Mary McSpadden
848	Dec. 8, 1809	Aaron Cate to Margaret Hull
849	Jan. 27, 1809	James Holland to Rebecca Hammond
850	June 26, 1809	Daniel Coffman to Kittie Dameron
851	Oct. 31, 1809	Isaac Newman to Eleanor Campbell
852	Nov. 21, 1809	David White to Betsey Ocheltree
853	Aug. 19, 1809	Isaac Cox to W. Austin
854	Aug. 1, 1809	George Baker to Margaret Miller
855	Jan. 31, 1809	Shadrack Goan to Sythey Inman
856	May 18, 1809	David Russell to Nancy Reeves
857	March 16, 1809	William Kimbro to Elizabeth Molden
858	March 27, 1809	Henry Derrick to Catherine Franner
859	Sept. 29, 1809	John Rightsell to Rebecca Phillips
860	March 17, 1809	Wilson Ore to Elizabeth Combs
861	March 18, 1809	James Snow to Nancy Riggs
862	May 10, 1809	Simon Adamson to Sarah Cox
863	Aug. 16, 1809	Stephen Churchman to Levica Smith
864	June 9, 1809	James Parmore to Polly Fowler
865	Jan. 4, 1809	John M. Hill to Elizabeth Copeland
866	Jan. 14, 1809	Job. Combs to Sarah Jones
867	April 19, ___	Berry Mitchell to Betsy Reeder
868	Aug. 4, 1809	Pleasant Garret to Margaret Beavard (Brevard)
869	Jan. 25, 1809	John Witt to Susannah Walker
870	April 1, 1809	John Leay to Elizabeth McClanahan

JEFFERSON COUNTY MARRIAGES

871	Jan. 25, 1809	John Prewitt to Rachel Wilson
872	Jan. 22, 1809	P. Sutton to Jane Dunlap
873	April 1, 1809	Amos Thomes to Mary Roak
874	Jan. 18, 1809	James Solomon to Jane Ferrand
875	March 3, 1809	Joshua Newman to Polly Lennox
876	Nov. 1, 1809	Jacob Eller to Elizabeth Winterbowers
877	Dec. 4, 1809	Benj. Harrison to Polly Lanston
878	Sept. 12, 1809	David Pierce to Sarah White
879	April 1, 1809	David Thornton to Mary Knave
880	Feb. 15, 1809	William Davis to Patsy Pucket
881	May 10, 1809	Nathan Shelly Jr. to Leah Neal
882	June 28, 1809	Joel Woods to Mary Sellers
883	April 12, 1810	Thomas Johnson to Martha Prewitt
884	April 12, 1810	Elisha Harrell to Mary Stanback (Stanbuck)
885	Oct. 14, 1810	Hampton Bales to Jane Bryson
886	April 12, 1810	Jacob Coppuck to Martha Elmore
887	Dec. 20, 1810	Robert Page to Elizabeth Bruce
888	April 4, 1810	John Duncan to Mary Henry
889	Nov. 16, 1810	Joseph Moore to Eliza Frazer
890	March 12, 1810	John Gwinn to Charity Mills
891	Jan. 30, 1810	Allen Bryan to Elizabeth McSpadden
892	July 7, 1810	Wm. Duncan to Jennet Brooks
893	Dec. 31, 1810	Edward Daur to Lydia Wilson
894	Aug. 22, 1810	Thomas Curry to Elizabeth Curry
895	April 7, 1810	B. Conyers to Sarah Witt
896	May 1, 1810	Daniel Meals to Mary Ann Cofman
897	Oct. 22, 1810	Isaac McClannahan to Francis Brown
898	Dec. 11, 1810	Jacob Sehorn to Hannah Wilson
899	Oct. 10, 1810	James Phagan to Elizabeth Pangle
900	Nov. 1, 1810	David McClannahan to Elizabeth Dellis
901	Oct. 23, 1810	Robert Williams to Rebecca Scoke
902	Dec. 26, 1810	Wm. McCullock to Ailey Willhelm
903	Sept. 13, 1810	T. Canon to Charlotte Copland
904	July 26, 1810	Daniel Lyle to Mary M. McGuire
905	Nov. 8, 1810	Jno. Perriman to Elizabeth Henderson
906	Dec. 10, 1810	Jno. Reay (Peay) (Read) to Sally Harvey
907	March 30, 1810	Hugh Key to Polly Atkins
908	March 9, 1810	Jesse Cheek to Susannah Pangle
909	April 7, 1810	Jacob Peck to Sophia Talbott
910	Sept. 6, 1810	James Dawces (Davces) (Davis) to Elizabeth McCullah
911	Sept. 13, 1810	Jesse Moore to Charlotte Copeland
912	Aug. 29, 1810	Jacob Black to Peggy Sellers
913	June 20, 1810	George Harris to Polly Craig
914	June 20, 1810	Jonathan Hall to Sarah Fortress
915	Aug. 23, 1810	Callowan Hodges to Amee Turner
916	Jan. 9, 1810	Allen Puckett to Betsey Britain

917	Aug. 1, 1810	George Walters to Mary Layman
918	Aug. 7, 1810	Samuel Evans to Elizabeth McCullah
919	Sept. 12, 1810	Nathan Turner to Patsy Haburg
920	Oct. 28, 1811	Enos Adamson to Jonna Stanley
921	Nov. 29, 1811	Charles Gordon to Polly Moore
922	April 11, 1811	Robert Cate to Patsey Jones
923	Aug. 2, 1811	David Williams and Hannah Pearce
924	Feb. 19, 1811	Chaney Moore to Patsey Allen
925	March 22, 1811	Richard Gresham to Milly Barns
926	Feb. 28, 1811	Jacob Storm to Delilah Howell
927	Dec. 5, 1811	William Henry to Sally Jones
928	June 6, 1811	Thomas Hanes to Sally Cheek
929	April 11, 1811	Habriel Lewes to Devota Spangler
930	Aug. 13, 1811	Christian Shrader to Mary Webb
931	Feb. 12, 1811	Mordica Reddin to Catherine Cox
932	Oct. 26, 1811	John Morris to Rachel Reece
933	Jan. 8, 1811	Joseph McGuire to Jane Collins
934	March 25, 1811	John Caldwell to Peggy Shadden
935	June 10, 1811	John Barnes to Polly Rodgers (Hodges)
936	Dec. 31, 1811	E. Lee to Polly Rogers (Rodgers)
937	Jan. 3, 1811	George Lowell to Susannah Copeland
938	Sept. 5, 1811	Thomas Cain to Rachel Harrison
939	July 22, 1811	Thomas Robinson to Sally King
940	Feb. ___ 1811	Samuel Hill to Elizabeth Canner
941	Nov. 16, 1811	Caleb Maye to Eliza Skein
942	Sept. 26, 1811	William Carson to Jane McGuffin
943	March 25, 1811	Elias Smith to C. McKinny
944	Aug. 1, 1811	Alex McGlocklin to Nancy Welsho
945	Dec. 13, 1811	B. Priddy (Preddy) to Susannah Moore
946	April 30, 1811	Andrew Campbell to Jane B. Campbell
947	April 20, 1811	John Hill to Jane Lyle
948	May 14, 1811	John Brymer to Anne Layman
949	Jan. 23, 1811	Eli Lewis to Rachel Holloway
950	Dec. 28, 1811	Thomas Pearce to Polly Steward
951	Feb. 27, 1811	Joshua Mayers (Moyers) to Mary Williams
952	Nov. 26, 1811	Thomas Nation to Deborah Hankins
953	Jan. 25, 1811	John Hanker to Priscilla Gridn
954	Jan. 30, 1811	Jesse Moore to Letty Rogers
955	Feb. 14, 1811	Samuel Hill to Polly Rice
956	March 15, 1811	James McLung to Jane Cameron
957	March 15, 1811	J. Jones to Mary Malcom
958	Aug. 20, 1811	Pulaski Wallace to Malinda Henderson
959	June 19, 1811	John Findley to Nancy Barne
960	April ___ 1811	Howell Cobb to Leah Williams
961	Oct. 19, 1811	John Carrol to Patsey Panson
962	Sept. 28, 1811	Joel Faircloth to Sarah McNeal
963	Nov. 26, 1811	James Hill to Margaret Cowan
964	Oct. 29, 1811	Enoch Lewis to Sally Campbell

965	Dec. 13, 1811	Moses Mills to Elizabeth Thornburgh
966	April 11, 1811	Nathaniel Cox to Elizabeth Talbott
967	June 24, 1811	Samuel Baker to Peggy McMean
968	July 12, 1811	Benj. Blake to Margaret Bradberry
969	June 23, 1811	Isaac Miles to Rachel Bales
970	July 16, 1811	William Brown to Elizabeth Lane
971	March 19, 1811	Williams Sims to Elizabeth Auts
972	June 26, 1812	T.W. Elliot to Hannah Morgan
973	April 1, 1812	Richard Manes to Nancy Johnson
974	July 27, 1812	George Pearce to Mary Hinchey
975	Dec. 17, 1812	Abraham Stropes to Sallie Tharp
976	Aug. 31, 1812	William Jones to Rebecca Ellis
977	Feb. 18, 1812	Richard Saunders to Tabitha Martin
978	Sept. 18, 1812	John Morris to Sara Stephenson
979	May 28, 1812	David Givens to Nancy Grace
980	Oct. 14, 1812	John Myers to Mary Snoddy (might be Moyers)
981	April 4, 1812	Joseph Breaden to Francis Copeland
982	July 11, 1812	John Dolen to Jennis Cates
983	Sept. 12, 1812	William Wood to Jane Henderson
984	Jan. 8, 1812	Andrew Coffman to Nancy Legg
985	July 4, 1812	Joshua Moore to Nancy McGuire
986	Sept. 1, 1812	John Cooper to Susannah _____
987	Feb. 19, 1812	Alexander Biggs to Isabella Rankin
988	Aug. 7, 1812	R. Lanmoore to Polly McFarland
989	Nov. 20, 1812	Abraham Dorrun to Patsy Holloway
990	Jan. 13, 1812	William Bearden to Delilah Perry
991	April 2, 1812	Isaac Clark to Jennena Webb
992	Feb. 1, 1812	John Slover to Rachel Taff
993	Nov. 12, 1812	James Wilhite to Peggy Baker
994	Oct. 5, 1812	David Weir to Elizabeth Henderson
995	Nov. 7, 1812	William Middleton to Betsy Davis
996	Nov. 21, 1812	Rolin Royers to Edie Brown
997	Aug. 19, 1812	James McDolaid to Rebecca _____
998	Aug. 4, 1812	John Bryson to Anne Bates
999	Jan. 23, 1812	Stephen Daniel to Patsy Davis
1000	Oct. 10, 1812	William McCarter to Sallie Brimer
1001	June 29, 1812	Abraham Adamson to Nelly Lewes
1002	May 18, 1813	William Howard to Fanny Moore
1003	Sept. 7, 1812	John Prewitt to Elizabeth Tucker
1004	Jan. 6, 1812	W.R. Panky to Nancy Baker
1005	Jan. 28, 1812	Wm. Brooks to Ailey Cantell (Cantrell)
1006	Dec. 3, 1812	John Willis to Lidie Swann (Swain)
1007	May 20, 1812	John Clendenen to Catherine Clark
1008	June 9, 1812	John Brimer to Sally Parrott
1009	Aug. 6, 1812	John Robinson to Ruth Shanks
1010	Jan. 29, 1812	Wm. Webb to Rebecca Bowen
1011	Feb. 1, 1812	John Forman to Anny Moore
1012	Jan. 28, 1812	Joel Denton to Jane Armstrong
1013	Feb. 14, 1812	Floyd McGangal to Nancy Mills
1014	July 23, 1812	Benj. Inman to Dorcas Doherty

1015	Aug. 6, 1812	John Mitchel to Patsy Bunch
1016	Maroh 30, 1812	W.T. Northern to Jane Howard
1017	April 13, 1812	T. Barnes to Elizabeth Harrison
1018	Nov. 25, 1812	Zack Clay to Susannah Horman (Harman)
1019	Sept. 25, 1812	James Carter to P. Carter
1020	Oct. 1, 1812	John Gentry to Priscilla Graham
1021	March 28, 1812	A. Lane to Polly Hailey
1022	Nov. 28, 1812	Joseph Cofman to Sally Meals
1023	Jan. 15, 1812	John Hash to Any Holloway
1024	Nov. 3, 1812	Wm. Milliken to Rebecca Elmore
1025	Aug. 1, 1812	Joseph Gresham to Sally Hill
1026	March 28, 1812	Geo. Laminore to Polly Riggs
1027	Sept. 9, 1812	James Gallahon to Allie Blackstone
1028	July 23, 1812	Wilson Cheek to Sally Anderson
1029	July 28, 1812	Silas Witt to Susannah Randolph
1030	July 28, 1812	Samuel Mathews to Sallie Barnett
1031	Aug. 10, 1812	Wm. Bunch to Nannie Bingham
1032	May 16, 1812	James Ritchie to Polly Willoughby
1033	May 9, 1812	Joseph Churchman to Polly Brittain
1034	Aug. 24, 1812	John Henderson to Dorcus McSpadden
1035	Jan. 6, 1812	John Cox to Rachel Sutherland
1036	Aug. 13, 1812	Andrew Gass to Polly Moyers
1037	Sept. 12, 1812	Robert Hood to Sally Albert
1038	May 6, 1812	James Doherty to Dicey Magers
1039	July 15, 1812	Joseph Miller to Betsey Moore
1040	Aug. 4, 1812	Wm. David to Jeremiah Riley
1041	May 5, 1812	Harvey Blackstone to Nancy Gallihime
1042	March 7, 1812	Wm. Bales to Elizabeth Adamson
1043	Nov. 28, 1812	John Anderson to Polly Simms
1044	Oct. 24, 1812	Jno. Prackett to Sally Thomas
1045	Oct. 16, 1812	John Maxwell to Hannah Haworth
1046	Dec. 15, 1813	John Mount to Sally Cates
1047	Feb. 25, 1813	James Cate to Elizabeth Linsey
1048	July 24, 1813	Solomon Prince to Elizabeth ____
1049	June 12, 1813	John McNight to Elender ____
1050	Aug. 15, 1813	Thomas Bryant to Nancy Cate
1051	Feb. 2, 1813	Jacob Miller to Betsy Edwards
1052	May 8, 1813	Andrew Neeley to Elizabeth McClanahan
1053	Jan. 12, 1813	Thomas Neugin to Pheba Cates
1054	Jan. 20, 1813	Jual Saunders to Polly Middlelin
1055	Dec. 27, 1813	James Bishop to Sarah Laurance
1056	March 27, 1813	Nicholas Long to Nancy White
1057	Nov. 14, 1813	Alexander McClannahan to Sally Claners
1058	April 14, 1813	John M. Pattin to Grizzy Moyers
1059	Dec. 20, 1813	Jacob Lyman to Sarah Aley
1060	Dec. 10, 1813	Frederick Pulse to Polly Wistly
1061	July 27, 1813	Patrick Dewoody to Easter B. McSpadden
1062	May 12, 1813	Chnsie Lyman to Elizabeth Brimer

1063	June 7, 1813	John Hays to Lyde Hoins
1064	June 8, 1813	P. Simmons to Rebecca Mills
1065	Nov. 6, 1813	Ephram Moore to Nancy Lane
1066	July 22, 1812	John Southerland to Mary Woodard
1067	March 20, 1813	Hezekiah Reneau to Tutha Brimer
1068	Jan. 19, 1813	Hugh McGuffin to Jenny Ford
1069	Dec. 2, 1813	Abraham Bams to M. Coppuck
1070	Dec. 13, 1813	Thomas Cofman to Jennet Kirkpatrick
1071	Oct. 1, 1813	Simon Wise to Nancy Right
1072	Aug. 2, 1813	Nathan Sellers to Ziphin Hodges
1073	April 30, 1813	Enoch Willongskley to Susannah Myers
1074	May 30, 1813	Alva James to Rebeca Hodges
1075	Nov. 6, 1813	John Thornburg to Polly Lay
1076	March 16, 1813	Benj. Henry to Elizabeth Hammel
1077	March 2, 1813	Edward Thommins to Elizabeth Ore
1078	Sept. 7, 1813	Michael Hanes to Elizabeth Kelly
1079	March 14, 1813	John Galbraith to Sally M. Fields
1080	July 19, 1813	Wm. Holeway to Peggy Draper
1081	July 17, 1813	Abraham Canator to Polly Peek
1082	Jan. 20, 1813	Wm. David to Rhoda Smith
1083	Aug. 9, 1813	Peter Simons to Rachel Mills
1084	May 13, 1813	Wm. Bragg to Melvina McGhee
1085	Aug. 5, 1813	Richard Longacre to Elizabeth Longacre
1086	Oct. 25, 1813	John Baker to Susannah Miller
1087	Feb. 2, 1813	Alexander Greenlee to Lida Smith
1088	Sept. 1, 1813	Jeremiah Walker to Christeny Clintz
1089	April 17, 1813	John Lennox to Catherine Roberts
1090	Jan. 12, 1813	James Todd to Elizabeth Taylor
1091	Jan. 28, 1813	Thomas Moore to Polly Cox
1092	March 10, 1813	Abraham McCarter to Nancy Brimer
1093	March 13, 1813	John W. Henderson to Nancy Molden
1094	Sept. 1, 1813	Wm. Stansberry to Polly Walker
1095	March 3, 1813	E. Hurley to Polly Cotney
1096	Oct. 16, 1813	William Bolden to Mary Drinnen
1097	April 12, 1813	John Douglass to Nancy Ritchey
1098	Jan. 22, 1813	John McClanahan to Nancy
1099	June 15, 1813	Isaac Harris to Elizabeth Pangle
1100	March 5, 1813	George Reneau to Polly Thomas
1101	Sept. 15, 1813	W. Ester to Lucy Rodgers
1102	Sept. 3, 1813	Thomas Shellin to Rebecca Daniel
1103	June 14, 1813	Wm. Mashill to Pheba Hann
1104	Aug. 31, 1813	A. Caldwell to Isabella Shadden
1105	Oct. 21, 1813	Wm. Simmons to Rebecca Sutherland
1106	May 3, 1813	Elijah Gresham to Betsey Terrill
1107	Oct. 29, 1813	Amon Baron to Nancy Riggs
1108	Aug. 31, 1813	Jacob G. Denton to Sally Armstrong
1109	Oct. 31, 1813	John Abel to Anne Gann
1110	Oct. 27, 1813	A.B. McFarland to Peggy M. Edgar
1111	June 26, 1813	Samuel Martain to Julia A. Reese
1112	Aug. 5, 1813	Vinyard Brimer to Barbara Lemmons
1113	Jan. 24, 1813	Joseph McCustin to Rachel McGuire
1114	April 3, 1813	David Witt to I. Skeen

1115	Jan. 2, 1813	Jonathan Thornburgh to Betsey Dernnis
1116	Aug. 20, 1814	Thomas Hickman to Sally Ward
1117	Sept. 3, 1814	Eli Shelton to Peggy Adamson
1118	Dec. 13, 1814	James Moore to H. Elder
1119	July 28, 1814	Isham Roberts to Edith Lucker
1120	Dec. 2, 1814	Robert Hodgen to Sallie Douglass
1121	Jan. 8, 1814	John Hornback to Nancy Howard
1122	Jan. 22, 1814	J. W. Hanly to Sally Carper
1123	Aug. 8, 1814	Wm. Mills to Martha Frager
1124	July 16, 1814	Aaron Mills to Nancy Wise
1125	June 14, 1814	John Campbell to Polly Selfhennir
1126	June 23, 1814	A. Gann to Nancy McGuire
1127	Oct. 26, 1814	Benj. Smith to Kittie Staples
1128	Aug. 17, 1814	Samuel Woodard to Abby Shelly
1129	May 29, 1814	George Seahorn to H. Hoskins
1130	March 9, 1814	James Graham to Sally McGirk
1131	May 2, 1814	Alex. McDonald to Polly McClister
1132	Oct. 29, 1814	Joel Smith to Priscilla Alexander
1133	Dec. 27, 1814	Thomas Comish to Polly Davis
1134	Nov. 8, 1814	Abraham Frazer to Peggy Coppock
1135	Nov. 20, 1814	Andrew Scott to Polly McGirt
1136		Charon Cheek to Jennie Anderson
1137	April 15, 1814	Enoch Witt to Peggy Pangler
1138	Feb. 14, 1814	Silas Henry to Paggy Neely
1139	Dec. 3, 1814	Wm. Walter to Betsey Horan
1140	March 9, 1814	Baxton Mitchell to Fanny Howard
1141	March 26, 1814	John Hill to P. Clark
1142	Oct. 2, 1814	William Beatis to Manah Jacobs
1143	Oct. 4, 1814	Wm. McKinney to Dandridge Todd
1144	Aug. 1, 1814	Jonathan Newman to Polly Lockhart
1145	Nov. 26, 1814	Robert Hueely to Gartery Cox
1146	March 12, 1814	Thomas Hale to Penna Lane
1147	Oct. 13, 1814	Wm. Crookshank to Sally McSpadden
1148	Oct. 29, 1814	Isaac Lowery to Jane Armstrong
1149	April 18, 1814	Silas Gentry to P. Witt
1150	July 18, 1814	Lemuel Mazc to Lucy M. Love
1151	Jan. 12, 1814	Joseph Duncan to Mary Howard
1152	Nov. 23, 1814	James Witt to Sally Cate
1153	Dec. 27, 1814	Abraham Solimon to Margaret Long
1154	Nov. 2, 1814	Samuel Jacobs to Sally Crider
1155	Jan. 22, 1814	Jacob Pate to Polly Bates
1156	Dec. 20, 1814	John McNiel to Polly Smith
1157	June 8, 1814	Robt. Swann to Rachel Cowan
1158	July 19, 1814	David Rankin to _____
1159	Sept. 1, 1814	Michael Branner to Edith Leath
1160	Nov. 30, 1814	Edmond Bell to Elizabeth Watkins
1161	June 1, 1814	James Will to Polly Hewn
1162	Nov. 11, 1814	Robert Rowen to Vnus Blair
1163		John Brittain to Easter Lain
1164	Sept. 17, 1814	Floyd Easter to A. Lea
1165	Feb. 17, 1814	Bird Pate to Rebecca Hankins
1166	June 30, 1814	William Cox to C. Austen
1167	May 13, 1814	Jesse Garland to Ruth Smith

1168	Aug. 10, 1814	Samuel Howard to Peggy Moore
1169	Dec. 2, 1815	George Walker to Elizabeth Nail
1170	June 1, 1815	Joshua Covey to Lydia Adamson
1171	June 1, 1815	Jacob Adamson to Ruthey Covey
1172	Sept. 19, 1815	Anderson Parkes to Cantrell (L. Cantrell)
1173	Aug. 28, 1815	James Anderton to Polly Cantrell
1174	March 13, 1815	Jonathan Hammer to Lidia Bayless
1175	Oct. 19, 1815	L. Romines to Nancy Robard
1176	March 4, 1815	Elisha Moore to Polly McClanahan
1177	Dec. 9, 1815	Wm. Wilson to Hester Adamson
1178	July 10, 1815	John Banton to Letitia Cate
1179	Feb. 11, 1815	John Rankin to Ruth McGair (McGuire)
1180	July 24, 1815	Wm. Moore to Jannie Miller
1181	July 4, 1815	Jonathan Howard to Daty Page
1182	March 4, 1815	John Banner to Jane Findley
1183	May 30, 1815	Wm. Faulkner to Hannah Morris
1184	March 18, 1815	David Gass to Nancy Branston
1185	Dec. 4, 1815	Thomas Roddick to Elizabeth Line
1186	Sept. 22, 1815	Thomas K. Clergyman to Dianna Carter
1187	Dec. 11, 1815	David Ashmore to Polly Shadden
1188	May 30, 1815	James Gass to Elizabeth Vandyke
1189	June 3, 1815	Isaac Todd to Naney Meals
1190	May 2, 1815	James Walker to Newey Williams
1191	Feb. 5, 1815	Charles Rooy to Darkie Daniel
1192	Dec. 19, 1815	Wm. Smith to Lidia Malcom
1193	Oct. 3, 1815	Joseph Adamson to Alsey Adamson
1194	Oct. 31, 1815	James Corbett to Polly Grisham
1195	Oct. 3, 1815	Wm. Lea to Susannah Pangle
1196	Nov. 1, 1815	S. Hall to Lear Lane
1197	Dec. 17, 1815	Adam Bane to Elizabeth Loury
1198	Sept. 11, 1815	James Goins to Peggy Midget
1199	Oct. 9, 1815	James Churchman to Nancy Bradberry
1200	Aug. 12, 1815	John Hodges to Jane Pucket
1201	Oct. 23, 1815	Wm. Copeland to Elizabeth Taff
1202	Nov. 17, 1815	James McClanahan to Manala Taylor
1203	July 2, 1815	William Kelley to Sallie Gray
1204	June 13, 1815	Elijah Moore to Rhoda Handy
1205	Sept. 11, 1815	Jeremiah Neal to Rachel Mapes
1206	Sept. 11, 1815	John Hartgraves to Jean McClister
1207	Sept. 20, 1815	John Gusham (Grisham) to Polly R. Corbett
1208	July 13, 1815	William N. Hoskin to Polly Branson
1209	Aug. 30, 1815	John Kimbro to Nanny Kimbro
1210	May 9, 1815	Charles Cobb to Catherine Curry
1211	Sept. 11, 1815	David Reese to Polly Donaldson
1212	May 29, 1815	John Roddy to Elizabeth Lane
1213	July 19, 1815	Samuel Reaves to Patsey Barnett
1214	Feb. 3, 1815	James Blackstone to Mary Bittle
1215	May 30, 1815	John Day to Fanny Holloway
1216	Feb. 13, 1815	Clement Nance to Peggy Nance

1217	March 3, 1815	George Lewis to Polly Swann
1218	May 6, 1815	Wm. Michael to Hannah Sellers
1219	June 22, 1815	John Toungn to Nancy Oten (Outen)
1220	April 26, 1815	G. Williams to Hilly Meadows
1221	Feb. 28, 1815	J. Middleton to Sally Rolston
1222	March 24, 1815	Z. Mills to Ann Woodard
1223	March 23, 1815	Eli Mills to Jane Patterson
1224	March 14, 1815	Peter Harrison to Jenny Rodgers
1225	Jan. 17, 1815	David Beates to Nancy Carmen
1226	March 11, 1815	Jeremiah Jones to Edith Edwards
1227	Feb. 5, 1815	Michael Grisham to Martha Corbet
1228	April 24, 1815	Isaac Rodgers to Sally Rodgers
1229	Jan. 11, 1815	Hiram Beazley to Kitty Arnold
1230	Dec. 25, 1816	Thomas Mansfield to Catherine McCustin
1231	Nov. 28, 1816	Wm. U. Williams to Hannah Frazer
1232	Oct. 15, 1816	Joseph Long to Sallie Pangle
1233	Oct. 2, 1816	John Handy to Elizabeth Hays
1234	April 19, 1816	Benj. Peck to K. McSpadden
1235	Feb. 15, 1816	James Galbraith to Patsy Hoskins
1236	Dec. 31, 1816	Joseph Talbott to Sally Rinehart
1237	Nov. 28, 1816	Charles White to C. Mills
1238	Sept. 25, 1816	Isaac Maxwell to Elizabeth Grooms
1239	Feb. 3, 1816	Isaac Horner to Polly Johnson
1240	Sept. 16, 1816	John R. Hornback to Polly Petty
1241	Dec. 19, 1816	Wm. Hickman to Susannah Minut
1242	April 20, 1816	John George to Elizabeth Welsh
1243	Jan. 9, 1816	Parker Everett to Aly Thornburgh
1244	March 21, 1816	James Simpson to Millie Price
1245	May 22, 1816	James Simpson to Millie Price
1246	April 21, 1816	Moses Skeen to Susannah Hardy
1247	July 13, 1816	Henry Selvege to Dice Jenneway
1248	June 9, 1816	Wm. Atkinson to Fanny Copeland
1249	March 1, 1816	Wm. Brazelton to Polly Reece
1250	Nov. 26, 1816	Thomas Ellis to Lydia Thornburgh
1251	Jan. 3, 1816	John Copeland to Susannah Sewell
1252	Sept. 2, 1816	Nathan Curry to Jennie Snow
1253	Aug. 20, 1816	Andrew B. Edgar to Elizabeth B. Handerson
1254	Dec. 27, 1816	James Reeves to A. McAndrew
1255	Nov. 20, 1816	F. Renno to Sallie Walters
1256	Nov. 7, 1816	James McClister to Sarah Reams
1257	March 13, 1816	Alexander Newman to Peggy Ashmore
1258	Aug. 28, 1816	Wm. Walker to Rebecca Coffman
1259	Nov. 6, 1816	Thomas Sparker to Sally McClister
1260	July 18, 1816	Wm. Daniel Jr. to Elizabeth West
1261	March 30, 1816	Thomas Hathcocke to Anna Robinson
1262	April 11, 1816	Wm. Kelly to Ruthy Munick
1265	April 20, 1816	Kimble Mudkipp to Nancy Perkupile
1266	June 4, 1816	James Shelton to Jane Langdon
1267	Dec. 11, 1816	Jacob Barnes to Peggy Danil
1268	Oct. 12, 1816	James Johnston to Patsy Skeen
1269	July 27, 1816	Philip Cother to Francis Staples
1270	Oct. 8, 1816	Moses Hodges to Jane Rogers

1271	Oct. 12, 1816	Robert McFarland to Hannah Barton
1272	Oct. 12, 1816	C. Brewer to Peggy Royston
1273	Dec. 19, 1816	John Taff to Scynthia Moore
1274	Sept. 3, 1816	John Denwoody to Polly Taylor
1275	Nov. 11, 1816	Robert Rodden to Unia Blair
1276	Nov. 18, 1816	James Biggs to Mary Gwinn
1277	March 26, 1816	John Larrance to Ruthy Mills
1278	April 5, 1816	Hezekiah Morgan to Lydia Hammer
1279	July 20, 1816	Adam Peck to Eliza Peck
1280	Aug. 28, 1816	Martin Caontrell to Susannah McDowell (Cantrell)
1281	April 15, 1816	John Smith to Sally Moore
1282	July 13, 1816	Levi Carter to Elizabeth Howard
1283	Sept. 18, 1816	Wadlington Wall to Polly Hickman
1284	Oct. 12, 1816	James Clark to Sally Bell
1285	Feb. 12, 1816	Wm. Watkins to Martha Barenger (Balinger)
1286	Sept. 25, 1816	John Rickets to Jane Vance
1287	Jan. 4, 1817	John Pangle to Easther Lane
1288	Feb. 29, 1817	Hugh Graham to Catharine Nenner
1289	Nov. 4, 1817	Andrew L. Henderson to Peggy McSpadden
1290	July 27, 1817	John Noah to Phoeby Cox
1291	Jan. 16, 1817	Alexander Edgar to Jane Felknor
1292	April 21, 1817	Wm. Givins to Priscilla Maze
1293	July 28, 1817	John McCampbell to Catharine Caldwell
1294	Aug. 7, 1817	Wm. Thornburgh to Patsy Bradshaw
1295	May 23, 1817	Noah Lane to Levice Taylor
1296	Aug. 11, 1817	James Weese to Nancy Eslinger
1297	Feb. 6, 1817	Robert Lyles to Dolly Copeland
1298	Aug. 3, 1816	Wm. Canhoozer to C. Thomas
1299	Oct. 22, 1817	John Norwood to Ruth Kilpatrick
1300	July 16, 1817	Andrew Falkenburg to Betsy Newman
1301	June 3, 1817	N. Manning to Mary Parrot
1302	Sept. 16, 1817	A. Thornburgh to Mary Landrum
1303	Dec. 17, 1817	Hugh Sehorn to Tabitha Ann Owens
1304	Feb. 15, 1817	Isaac I. Watkins to Peggy Reese
1305	Nov. 1, 1817	Isaah Coffman to Ellender Hill
1306	Nov. 20, 1807 (1817)	Thomas J. Campbell to Sallie L. Bearden
1307	Aug. 12, 1817	Samuel Fain to Peggy Campbell
1308	Nov. 13, 1817	Richard Luttrell to Mary Tunley
1309	Aug. 2, 1817	Reuben Thomas to Polly Dellis
1310	July 26, 1817	Thomas Bimbro to Anne Smith(Kimbro)
1311	April 15, 1817	Michael Barnet to Ester Daniel
1312	Jan. 13, 1817	George W. Pulse to Kalley Kamebrer
1313	July 16, 1817	Thomas Sawett to Nancy Layman
1314	Sept. 17, 1817	James Taff to Hannah Hill
1315	July 3, 1817	Barton Samith to Ealbey Moore
1316	July 3, 1817	Thomas Oliver to Susan Hacket
1317	Nov. 1, 1817	Wiley Woods Jr. to Frankie Sassern
1318	Sept. 22, 1817	Joseph Easter to Rebecca Bennett
1319	April 5, 1817	Joseph Easter to Polly Smith

JEFFERSON COUNTY MARRIAGES

1320	Nov. 22, 1817	Abel Wilson to Rebecca Stubbleffeld
1321	Nov. 22, 1817	N. Chamberlan to Margaret Watkins
1322	Oct. 16, 1817	Thomas Horner to Catherine Helton
1323	Aug. 29, 1817	John Royer to Margaret Denton
1324	Feb. 6, 1817	Samuel McSpadden to Polly A. Lowery
1325	July 22, 1817	Silas Patterson to Guley Reneau
1326	Dec. 22, 1817	Herman Griffin to Anne Hensley
1327	April 1, 1817	Nathan Shelley to Jane Brazelton
1328	Sept. 13, 1817	Moses Barnes to Anne Lenox
1329	Sept. 22, 1817	George Herndon to Hannah Cox
1330	May 21, 1817	John Moore to Nancy Keeney
1331	Oct. 27, 1817	John Robertson to Sally Miller
1332	May 3, 1817	Wm. Hammonds to Hannah Frazier
1333	April 24, 1817	Richard Haynes to Susannah Mundenhall
1334	June 10, 1817	John Duinbee to Jenny Maples
1335	Feb. 1, 1817	Isaac Smith to Susannah Moore
1336	Aug. 7, 1817	Richard Breeden to Sally Locket
1337	March 11, 1817	Thomas Patterson to Anne Thornburgh
1338	Nov. 13, 1817	Gallant Hert to Susan McDonald
1339	May 10, 1817	C.H. Horner to Elizabeth Haun
1340	April 19, 1817	James Gardner to Nancy Meredith
1341	March 11, 1817	Henry Collins to Elizabeth Douglass
1342	Aug. 23, 1817	Wm. Vineyard to Katy Skeen
1343	Aug. 6, 1817	Dickson Cantrell to Susan Parker
1344	May 28, 1817	Wm. Brant (Bryant) to Lucy Kate (Cate)
1345	Nov. 5, 1818	Isaah Ballard to Lidia Prichard
1346	April 27, 1818	Thomas McKnight to A. Frazier
1347	June 25, 1818	Wm. Taylor to Anes Manes
1348	May 26, 1818	Tidence Lane to Catherine Pangle
1349	April 18, 1818	John Letner to Jennie Maples
1350	May 23, 1818	Wm. Taff to Sallie Copeland
1351	April 9, 1818	Thomas Baker to Nancy Gowan
1352	March 22, 1818	George W. Russell to Polly Newman
1353	June 29, 1818	Wm. Elmore to Nancy Northern
1354	Oct. 4, 1818	Jesse Fielding to Elizabeth Biggs
1355	April 4, 1818	Charles Hodge Jr. to Elisa Thompson
1356	Dec. 4, 1818	George Roupe to Margaret Baldwin
1357	March 19, 1818	Wm. Northern to Sally Blackburn
1358	Dec. 28, 1818	Zadock Riggs to Patsey Mays
1359	Jan. 6, 1818	James Falknor to Anne Guthne
1360	Aug. 17, 1818	Geo. R. Smith to Betsy White
1361	April 23, 1818	Charles Harrison to Sally Harle
1362	July 18, 1818	Daniel Horn to M. McDonald
1363	Sept. 7, 1818	Eli Bettis to Dolly Lewis
1364	May 2, 1818	Gearland Gear to Permelia Reed
1365	June 11, 1818	Richard Staples to Fanny Jones
1366	April 18, 1818	Wm. Gollaher to Betsey Thompson
1367	July 21, 1818	Samuel Howard to Frankey Blackburn
1368	March 21, 1818	George Curry to Polly Goen
1369	Sept. 22, 1818	John Inman to Catherine McFarland
1370	June 17, 1818	John Newman to Jane K. Caldwell
1371	Nov. 10, 1818	David Bowerman to Elizabeth Eaton

1372	March 18, 1818	Edward Sellars to Sally Witt
1373	Feb. 25, 1818	Wm. Taylor to Polly Lingerfeltor
1374	DEc. 30, 1818	Jacob Gure to Elizabeth Brown
1375	Aug. 25, 1818	Wm. McDowel to Polly Pearson
1376	Oct. 19, 1818	Wm. Doherty to Rosanna McDonald
1377	Oct. 10, 1818	Henry H. Peck to Eley Cox
1378	Dec. 15, 1818	Samuel Cox to Nancy Mullins
1379	Oct. 4, 1818	Wm. Doherty to Sally Hanes
1380	Jan. 20, 1818	Philip Watkins to Mary McDonald
1381	Feb. 26, 1818	John Russell to Nancy Ellis
1382	Jan. 25, 1818	H. Carey to Nancy Whalen
1383	Jan. 22, 1818	Abraham Hill to Patsey Walker
1384	May 21, 1818	Peter Thomas to Nancy Robertson
1385	March 28, 1818	Wm. Butery to Levice King
1386	Sept. 3, 1818	Wm. Prewet to Sally Pendleton
1387	Aug. 2, 1818	Benj. Hickman to Jenny Sharp
1388	Sept. 23, 1818	Stokley Tolls to L. Ward
1389	Jan. 12, 1818	James McCuistian to Nelly Grace
1390	June 27, 1818	Wm. Meals to Susannah Cofman
1391	Aug. 25, 1818	Wm. Moore to Polly Royer
1392	Dec. 17, 1818	Adam Bone to Elizabeth Lowry
1393	Dec. 11, 1818	Wm. Mendenhall to Jenny Gibbons
1394	April 15, 1818	Blair Newman to Margaret Coldwell (Caldwell)
1395	Feb. 2, 1818	Nathan Mills to Sarah Lawrence
1396	Jan. 12, 1818	Joseph Austen to Ailsey Curry
1397	Aug. 29, 1818	Samuel Douglas to Mary Sellars
1398	Jan. 28, 1818	George Graham to Catherine Wenton or Denton
1399	Sept. 10, 1818	Wm. Jett to Anna Mansfield
1400	Dec. 1, 1818	John Church to Polly Mansfield
1401	Feb. 2, 1818	John E. Cate to Polly Ferrell
1402	Nov. 9, 1818	George Leeth to Elizabeth Branner
1403	Nov. 17, 1818	John Bear to Polly Inman
1404	Dec. 31, 1818	Wm. A. Montgomery to Sarah Jarnagan
1405	May 3, 1818	Wm. Hamlet to Peggy Cluck
1406	April 29, 1818	Solomon Copeland to Nancy Putner
1407	Dec. 13, 1818	James Morris to Sally Bishop
1408	July 29, 1818	A. Skeen to Judah Brown
1409	Sept. 7, 1818	Laide Cooper to Rachel Cox
1410	Sept. 20, 1819	Jonathan Langdon to Elizabeth Taylor
1411	Sept. 4, 1819	Jacob Angle to Judah Welsh
1412	Nov. 13, 1819	Alex. Marshall to Aggy Dallas
1413	March 19, 1819	Thomas Rankin to Caroline Franklin
1414	Nov. 18, 1819	Ebenezer Fain to Mary Campbell
1415	Oct. 21, 1819	Noah Witt to J. Smith
1416	Sept. 25, 1819	David C. Fenley to Sally Langford
1417	Sept. 21, 1819	James Burgiss to Sessan Steard
1418	Dec. 23, 1819	Job Garretson to Winney Cooper
1419	Oct. 23, 1819	Hiram Shepard to Betsy Frank
1420	Oct. 4, 1819	Wm. Combs to Catherine Georgey
1421	April 18, 1819	George Rayl to Polly Cheek
1422	April 19, 1819	Joshua Nelson to Peggy Brimmer

1423	Dec. 4, 1819	Elisha Prewit to B. Horton
1424	Oct. 20, 1819	Isaac Maiden to Betsy Maiden
1425	July 19, 1819	James Mills to Naomi Churchman
1426	Dec. 17, 1819	Thomas Wilkerson to Sally Williams
1427	Sept. 5, 1819	Wm. Thompson to Jane Meek
1428	July 12, 1819	James Dodd to Milly Walker
1429	Jan. 28, 1819	Shadrack Inman to Sally K. Henderson
1430	March 31, 1819	Daniel Ogbourne to Polly Barnett
1431	Dec. 8, 1819	Thos. J. Martin to Polly Barnett
1432	Oct. 27, 1819	Robert Large to Patsy Dannel
1433	Aug. 5, 1819	John Grame to Mary Thornburgh
1434	July 7, 1819	Joel Mullins to Susannah Manley
1435	July 13, 1819	John Cate to Polly Mount
1436	Aug. 30, 1819	Wm. Dick to Sarah Blagg
1437	Feb. 11, 1819	John Blue to Polly Shield
1438	May 22, 1819	Jonathan Mills to Elizabeth Peck
1439	Oct. 31, 1819	Wm. Davidson to Eleanor Selvidge
1440	March 24, 1819	John Pearson to Lucinda Dyer
1441	May 15, 1819	Augustus Smith to Susan Humpston
1442	Nov. 11, 1819	John Longacre to Sylvy Hays
1443	Sept. 16, 1819	Lucas Kennedy to Elizabeth Hamilton
1444	Aug. 27, 1819	L. Flatfoot to Elizabeth Guinn
1445	April 19, 1819	Joel W. Cowen to Annis W. Inman
1446	Oct. 6, 1819	Wm. French to Casinbra Cantrell
1447	March __ 1819	James Nelson to Jenny Sarton (Barton)
1448	Aug. 30, 1819	Wm. Mills to Rebecca Sumers
1449	May 31, 1819	Daniel E. Becknell to Polly Fain
1450	Jan. 28, 1819	Solomon White to Nancy Bales
1451	Feb. 15, 1819	Jas. Hedrick to Martha Rodgers
1452	May 25, 1819	John C. Harvy to Patsy Adams
1454	March 12, 1819	John Blowons to Polly Parrott
1455	Oct. 5, 1819	Moses Roberts to Kesiah Guinn
1456	Nov. 16, 1819	David Lichliter to Polly Rhineheart
1457	Jan. 8, 1819	Martin Brooks to Betsy Young
1458	Feb. 13, 1819	Jesse Mills to Susannah Hamlet
1459	Feb. 10, 1819	Alex Hill to Dandridge McKinney
1460	May 3, 1819	Isaac Curry to Fanny Mays
1461	Aug. 31, 1819	Daniel Campbell to Susan Goens
1462	Jan. 15, 1819	Henry Thomas to Sally Branner
1463	Feb. 7, 1819	James Oates to Betsy Wilhite
1464	Oct. 8, 1819	John Lanson to Lucy Shewheard
1465	Nov. 18, 1819	John C. Eckle to Mary Gigar
1466	Feb. 3, 1819	Jacob Benton (Denton) Jr. to Deborah Lichliter
1467	Sept. 6, 1819	Thomas Russell to Jane Greene
1468	March 26, 1819	Allen Sarrete to Isabella Sinnell
1469	March 29, 1819	John Bales to Betsy Lewes
1470	Sept. 13, 1819	Patrick Hale to Sidnah Roddy
1471	March 1, 1819	Henry Giger to Nancy Todd
1472	Feb. 17, 1819	Wm. Doherty to Peggy Denton
1473	Jan. 26, 1819	James McQuster to Elizabeth Gussam
1474	Feb. 9, 1820	Robt. A. Scott to Nancy Smiley
1475	Aug. 23, 1820	John Ritchey to Betsy Williams

1476	Dec. 16, 1820	John Tucker to Betsey Bennet
1477	Dec. 19, 1820	Henry Lawrence to Nancy Tharp
1478	Aug. 10, 1820	Robt. McFarland to Polly Ann Scott
1479	Jan. 21, 1820	James Blackburn to Sarah Adkinson
1480	Oct. 14, 1820	Thomas Deweese to Lavinia Thornburg
1481	March 7, 182-	Andrew Bare to Priscilla E. Doherty
1482	June 12, 1820	Elijah Sims to Susannah Spoon
1483	March 11, 1820	James Sutliff to Hannah Ailey
1484	June 11, 1820	Joseph Lackey to Priscilla Nugent
1485	March 13, 1820	Nicholas Coffman to Nancy Thomas
1486	Jan. 25, 1820	Elijah Mann to N. Bell
1487	May 16, 1820	Robert P. Craig to Nancy Sutliff
1488	May 13, 182-	David Gilliland to Fanny Quolls
1489	Aug. 12, 1820	Isaac Moore to Lucinda Harris
1490	Jan. 8, 1820	John Smith to Priscilla May
1491	Feb. 5, 1820	Wm. Cox to Peggy McDonald
1492	Dec. 23, 1820	Miles Jones to Mary Ann Quarles
1493	Feb. 25, 1820	David Kidwell to Polly Miller
1494	Dec. 18, 1820	John Mansfield to Margaret Ford
1495	July 3, 1820	Henry Chambers to Sarah Newman
1496	June 9, 1820	John Turner to S. Cate
1497	March 30, 1820	Elijah Cates to Susannah Underwood
1498	Sept. 4, 1820	Wm. McCory to Susannah Lewis
1499	May 10, 1820	George G. Satterfield to Anna Cluck
1500	Dec. 23, 1820	Gideon Cate to Elizabeth Stephenson
1501	June 3, 1820	Wm. John to Lidia Bales
1502	Oct. 7, 1820	Abner Snoddy (Snolly) to F. Fortenburg
1503	May 18, 1820	Barnet Smith to Betsey Manson
1504	Nov. 18, 1820	Elijah Parker to Mary McKnight
1505	Jan. 4, 1820	John Baker to Martha Mills
1506	Nov. 18, 1820	Abner Lile to Patsy Cate
1507	Aug. 23, 1820	John Ritchey to Betsy Williams
1508	Dec. 7, 1820	Wm. Cate to Betsey Mount
1509	Aug. 21, 1820	James P. Balch to Polly R. Edgar
1510	Aug. 18, 1820	Ely Wilson to Susannah Adamson
1511	June 13, 1820	John C. Burnett to Flora Henderson
1512	Nov. 17, 1820	George Harris to Julianna Harmon
1513	Nov. 23, 1820	Julius Blackwell to Mahala D. Liles
1514	June 11, 1820	Joseph Lackey to Priscilla Magnet
1515	March 1, 1820	Thomas Jacob to Elizabeth McGuire
1516	Jan. 4, 1820	James Johnson to Elizabeth Horner
1517	Aug. 24, 1820	Robert Adams to L. Harris
1518	Dec. 25, 1820	Joseph Large to Franky Childres
1519	March 13, 1820	David Gibbons to Sally Langford
1520	Jan. 3, 1820	George Cowan to Lydia Thornton
1521	Dec. 21, 1820	Walter Evans to Salina Hutchinson
1522	March 20, 1820	Wm. Simell to Mary Whalen
1523	Jan. 21, 1820	Henry Lewis to Mary Mills
1524	Dec. 27, 1820	Stephen Barker to Amanda Colvin
1525	March 8, 1820	Jacob Rodgers to Juliana Sampson
1526	Dec. 5, 1820	John Bragg to Esther Lichliter
1527	Sept. 18, 1820	John Evans to Susannah Worly
1528	Aug. 7, 1820	James Bankerston to Margaret Swan

1529	Feb. 23, 1820	Wm. Grant to Sally Holloway
1530	May 27, 1820	Francis Moser to Polly Scipe
1531	Feb. 1, 1820	Stephen Moore to B. Hackworth
1532	Sept. 2, 1820	Wm. Morrison to Margaret Griffin
1533	Oct. 31, 1820	A.P. Fore to Nancy Monroe
1534	Oct. 25, 1820	G. Watkins to Nancy Wiseman
1535	July 3, 1820	Holbert Arnot to Elizabeth Kirkpatrick
1536	Dec. 26, 1820	James Scribner to Hannah Ritchey
1537	March 8, 1820	Robert McFarland to Mary Weaver
1538	Jan. 23, 1820	Henry Counts to Mary Stubblefield
1539	Dec. 22, 1820	John Brown to Anny Smith
1540	Dec. 10, 1820	John Cartes (Cates) to Mary Embers (could be Carter)
1541	Feb. 21, 1820	John Lockhart to Mary Coppock
1542	March 11, 1820	James Sutliff to Hannah Ailey
1543	Sept. 1, 1820	Samuel Parker to Elinor McKnight
1544	April 20, 1820	Wm. Sartain to Polly Music
1545	April 29, 1820	Thomas Keeney to Sarah Moore
1546	Sept. 6, 1820	Wm. Carter to Sally Harriston
1547	Oct. 15, 1821	Henry H. Myers to Nancy McGowan
1548	Aug. 11, 1821	John Wolf to Elizabeth Franklin
1549	Nov. 24, 1821	John Wright to Sally Ferrell
1550	Jan. 18, 1821	Nolen Henderson to Polly Branner
1551	Nov. 17, 1821	John Childress to Rachel Clanahan
1552	Nov. 17, 1821	John Woods to Mary Owten
1553	Jan. 25, 1821	James Hamble to Betsy Newman
1554	July 24, 1821	Adam Dunwoody to Eliza Mooser
1555	Feb. 15, 1821	James Robinson to Rachel Chilton
1556	Nov. 15, 1821	Thomas Dryden to Eliza Carig
1557	Feb. 1, 1821	Jesse George to Rachel McFarland
1558	Jan. 23, 1821	Wm. Felton to Prudence McDonald
1559	April 14, 1821	Wm. White to Rosannah Thomas
1560	Jan. 23, 1821	Reuben Purkepile to Sally McGhee
1561	Nov. 13, 1821	John C. Smith to Scynthia DenWitt
1562	Nov. 5, 1821	Michael McGuire to Harriet Jacobs
1563	June 18, 1821	Adam K. Meek to Elizabeth Childres
1564	March 22, 1821	Samuel McSpadden to Jane Henderson
1565	Jan. 4, 1821	Joseph Woods to Sally Carson
1566	March 15, 1821	Charles Shubird to Lydia Thomas
1567	Jan. 21, 1821	Thomas Reid to Mary Chilton
1568	June 13, 1821	John B. Horner to Margaret McDonald
1569	Dec. 3, 1821	Wm. Kelly to Martha Gentry
1570	Aug. 10, 1821	Wm. Moser to Betsy Ealinger
1571	March 7, 1821	Thomas Rankin to Sally Ashmore
1572	Feb. 9, 1821	K. Moore to Polly Newman
1573	June 5, 1821	Laburn Curry to Polly Medkiff
1574	Oct. 1, 1821	Benj. McCrarey to M. Sampson
1575	July 11, 1821	Spencer Horner to Axey Robertson
1576	Dec. 1821	James Turk to Mary Markland
1577	Oct. 10, 1821	Samuel Brazelton to Mary Lawrence
1578	Jan. 23, 1821	Reuben Prukepile to Sally McGhee
1579	Aug. 10, 1821	Adam M. Kennedy to Betsy D. Ritchey
1580	Feb. 20, 1821	Robt. Covey to Anna Todd

1581	April 8, 1821	George Branner to Mary Ann Roper
1582	July 6, 1821	Wm. Bales to Elizabeth Williams
1583	Jan. 6, 1821	Jesse Riggs to Mary Henderson
1584	Nov. 20, 1821	Nicholas Long and Hannah Churchman
1585	June 13, 1821	Wm. Edkins to Mary A. Davis
1586	Nov. 27, 1821	Henry Hanner to Francis Perkins
1587	Oct. 11, 1821	Jacob Large to Betsy Dinnel
1588	April 8, 1821	John Whalen to Dolly Liles
1589	Dec. 25, 1821	Allen Stone to Polly Armes
1590	Dec. 22, 1821	Solomon Frazier to Anna Russell
1591	June 9, 1821	James Clark to P. Davis
1592	Nov. 25, 1821	George Wray to Hannah Samples
1593	April 4, 1821	Augustus Rice to Mary McFarland
1594	July 21, 1821	Elisha Cate to Mary E. Newman
1595	Oct. 15, 1821	Cyrus McClure to U. Baker
1596	Oct. 26, 1821	David Thomas to Sally Mason
1597	Oct. 27, 1821	Randolph McGuin to Catherine Wray
1598	1821	Peter Taff to Elizabeth Atkinson
1599	March 21, 1821	Wm. Austin to Anna Hanes
1600	Dec. 10, 1821	James Stubblefield to Phebe Riggs
1601	Aug. 9, 1821	Silas B. Stephenson to Lavinia Mathes
1602	Jan. 28, 1821	John Dolan to Polly Jolly
1603	Jan. 24, 1821	Benj. Carr to Mary Vandike
1604	Sept. 17, 1821	Robt. Ritchey to Lavinca Miller
1605	July 16, 1821	Abel Rickets to Matilda Walton
1606	April 29(19)1821	Isaac Roddy to Mary Martin
1607	Jan. 26, 1821	John Crubb to Minney McDowell
1608	Sept. 20, 1821	John Balinger to Polly Berger
1609	Feb. 27, 1821	Wm. Mills to Nancy Hamlet
1610	Feb. 21, 1821	Wm. Henderson to Betsy Cowan
1611	May 31, 1822	Wm. Campbell to Peggy Blackburn
1612	Oct. 10, 1822	John Ritchey to Catharine Doherty
1613	Jan. 16, 1822	John Allen to Elizabeth Edwards
1614	Jan. 16, 1822	Nelson Griffin to Peggy Reese
1615	Aug. 23, 1822	Jesse Norman to Betsy Whalen
1616	Jan. 3, 1822	Elijah Cate to Nelly David
1617	Jan. 23, 1822	Henry Vandyke to Lucy Cates
1618	May 9, 1822	Robert Gaut to Polly P. Wood
1619	June 24, 1822	Wm. Hill to Mary Carmcle (Carmicheal)
1620	March 5, 1822	Hiram Russell to Elizabeth Cox
1621	June 19, 1822	Israel Patton to Hannah Mills
1622	May 30, 1822	John Green to Betsy Carmichael
1623	Dec. 19, 1822	Mordicai Adamson to Susannah Peck
1624	Jan. 3, 1823	James Garret to Elizabeth Helton
1625	Nov. 16, 1822	Isaac Rodgers to Celia Frederick
1626	May 16, 1822	Joab Blackwell to Sally Newman
1627	Aug. 17, 1822	Wm. Carman to Jane Milles
1628	Oct. 24, 1822	Lampkin McKinney to Catharine Staples
1629	June 7, 1822	Gardner Whalen to Betsy Day
1630	Feb. 3, 1822	M.L. Penkslow to A. Goforth
1631	Dec. 10, 1822	David Vance to Margaret Taylor

1632	Dec. 26, 1822	John Gaut to Margaret Burns
1633	June 4, 1822	John Larrence to Amy McCullock
1634	May 25, 1822	James Mitchell to Nancy Puckett
1635	Dec. 4, 1822	Samuel Cofman to Polly Lane
1636	May 27, 1822	Thomas Bettis to Mary Palmer
1637	July 27, 1822	Samuel Legg to Betsy Horner
1638	Feb. 18, 1822	James Newman to Isabella Rankin
1639	Feb. 1, 1822	Christopher Moyer to Sarah McGowan
1640	Dec. 22, 1822	Thomas Elmore to Elizabeth Neal
1641	March 9, 1822	Asa Howell to Elizabeth Talbott
1642	Nov. 13, 1822	Daniel R. Murphy to Lucy L. Carter
1643	Feb. 12, 1822	Benj. Canady to Anne Haworth
1644	Oct. 10, 1822	Adam Letner to Julian Mosses
1645	Jan. 2, 1822	Wm. Luttrell to Susannah Kerr
1646	Oct. 31, 1822	Thomas Denton to Elizabeth Denton
1647	July 15, 1822	Thomas Moreland to Peggy James
1648	Nov. 21, 1822	Wm. Bethel to Margaret Bruce
1649	Nov. 21, 1822	John H. Lea to Elizabeth A. Martin
1650	Feb. 27, 1822	James Bicknell to Fanny Hoskins
1651	Dec. 6, 1822	John Cook to Phebe Large
1652	April 10, 1822	John G. Staples to Phebe Burn
1653	Jan. 20, 1822	John Hickey to Betsy Grant
1654	Nov. 18, 1822	Mathew Cowan to Diana P. Burenine
1655	June 12, 1822	John Campbell to Peggy _____
1656	Nov. 6, 1822	Levi Morgan to Sarah Peck
1657	Oct. 21, 1822	Wm. Mills to Betsy Worley
1658	Aug. 29, 1822	Wm. M. Wilson to Elizabeth Talbott
1659	April 22, 1822	Joseph Grisham to Catherine McGuire
1660	Aug. 5, 1822	Alex. McGhee to Nancy D. Liles
1661	Oct. 15, 1822	Hiram Reynolds to Elizabeth Biggs
1662	Jan. 6, 1822	Baldwin Harle to Mary Lee (Lea)
1663	Feb. 13, 1822	Thomas Ritchey to Mary Ann Nelson
1664	Feb. 13, 1822	James North to Betsy Putman
1665	May 9, 1822	James L. Neal to Sarah M. Lanan
1666	Aug. 21, 1822	Thomas Kelly to Sallie Franklin
1667	Nov. 19, 1822	John N. Newman to Rebecca Grace (might be 1828)
1668	Sept. 4, 1822	Ephraim Dyer to Phebe Majors
1669	Dec. 31, 1822	Isaac Snodgrass to Nancy Long
1670	March 22, 1822	Solomon White to Polly Bales
1671	May 25, 1822	Jesse Dogget to Nancy McCown
1672	Oct. 1, 1822	Jas. Hamilton Jr. to Nancy Martin
1673	July 15, 1822	Nicholas N. Davis to Mary Landrum
1674	Aug. 11, 1822	James Ward to Nancy McKinney
1675	Jan. 22, 1822	Robert Vance to Joanna Ricket
1676	Jan. 14, 1822	Wm. McKinney to Margaret Laverly
1677	March 29, 1822	Wm. Hankins to Polly Cates
1678	Jan. 22, 1822	Jas. B. Woods to Polly L. Cannon
1679	May 27, 1822	Joel Duncan to Nancy Goforth
1680	Dec. 19, 1822	John Lockhart to Sarah Rankin
1681	Aug. 27, 1822	Nathaniel D. Ritchey to Rachel Brazelton
1682	Sept. 12, 1822	Averritt Ritter to Charlotte Smith
1683	Jan. 23, 1823	Wm. Thornburgh to Nancy Brister (Bruister)

1684	Feb. 3, 1823	John Mills to Nancy Churchman
1685	Sept. 6, 1823	Alexander Seahorn to Polly Long
1686	Oct. 7, 1823	Robt. Harvey to Nancy Adams
1687	Jan. 18, 1823	Levi Manard to Catherine French
1688	Jan. 15, 1823	John Burnet to Jane Cate
1689	May 12, 1823	John Cardwell to Araminta Watkins
1690	June 5, 1823	John Whittengler to Elizabeth Rankin
1691	March 10, 1823	Thomas Patterson to D. Kidwell
1692	Aug. 27, 1823	Wm. Hickman to Elizabeth Russell
1693	Nov. 8, 1823	Russell Crow to Patsy Howell
1694	Sept. 23, 1823	Claiburn Brown to Rebecca Briant
1695	Dec. 3, 1823	Larken Adamson to Nancy Routh
1696	Dec. 1823	Isaac L. J. Thompson to Jane Hamble
1697	Dec. 19, 1823	John Hickman to Ann Ward
1698	Feb. 18, 1823	James Wilmott to Frances McLanakan
1699	Aug. 20, 1823	John Myuck to Mary Burns
1700	Sept. 5, 1823	Thomas Glascow to Elizabeth Evans
1701	Jan. 15, 1823	Joseph Blagg to Mary Dick
1702	March 18, 1823	George Curry to Nancy West
1703	Nov. 24, 1823	Joseph Doherty to Patsy Wilmouth
1704	June 1, 1823	M. Reneau to Priscilla Denton
1705	June 10, 1823	Mathes Tague to Rebecca Collins (Teague)
1706	Oct. 21, 1823	Wm. Lamar to Rebecca Hodge
1707	June 4, 1823	John Bettis to Isabella Liles
1708	April 24, 1823	Joseph King to Eliza Hensley
1709	June 21, 1823	John Bowman to Mary Ann Brown
1710	July 19, 1823	Wm. Day to Susannah Carmichael
1711	March 6, 1823	John Hart to Jane Hodges
1712	Jan. 30, 1823	Wm. Burnet to Elenor Williams
1713	Aug. 21, 1823	Charles Chaney to Phebe Brown
1714	July 14, 1823	Nathan Cox to Sally Wheeler
1715	Feb. 12, 1823	James H. Caldwell to Catherine Blackburn
1716	Dec. 15, 1823	Samuel Bettis to Jemima Howell
1717	June 4, 1823	Abarham Childers to Eleanor Duerkin
1718	Aug. 17, 1823	Smallwood Middleton to Elizabeth Thornburgh
1719	May 24, 1823	Joseph White to Susannah Walker
1720	March 22, 1823	Nathaniel Flatfoot to Margaret Pearson
1721	June 20, 1823	Wm. Evans to Maria Couter
1722	Dec. 29, 1823	Nelson T. Combs to Sarah Talbot
1723	Jan. 30, 1823	John Mount to Patsy Mills
1724	March 3, 1823	Thos. Cantrell to Nancy McKee
1725	June 18, 1923	John Newman to Elizabeth Ashmore
1727	Aug. 25, 1823	West Haworth to Rebecca White
1728	Dec. 7, 1823	John King to Elizabeth Bell
1729	May 5, 1823	John Brown to Jane Kirkpatrick
1730	Oct. 7, 1823	Chester Jarnagin to Margaret Grove
1731	Oct. 19, 1823	Wm. Bunnells to Sarah White
1732	Dec. 11, 1823	Gray Garrett to Maria Harle
1733	June 6, 1823	Nathaniel Burnet to Elizabeth Oaks
1734	Aug. 7, 1823	John Hasket to Betsy Hegdon

1735	May 28, 1823	Ross Ralbertt (Talbott) to Temperance Howell
1736	Dec. 3, 1823	David Shaw to Mary Wyatt
1737	Dec. 29, 1823	Nelson Chilton to Fanny Sheppard
1738	Jan. 13, 1823	Reuben L. Humpston to Levina McClenahan
1739	Sept. 2, 1823	Joseph Kitrell to Mary Chambers
1740	July 29, 1823	Wm. Harris to Fanny Cartner
1741	Oct. 20, 1823	John Mopson to Sally McCrary
1742	Nov. 1, 1823	Robert Morgan to Betsy Latham
1743	Nov. 1, 1823	Darling Hogin to Lucinda Fry
1744	Nov. 7, 1823	Aaron Kelsey to Eleanor Givens
1745	Oct. 13, 1823	Walter Howell to Nancy Lawrence
1746	Feb. 16, 1823	John W. Jewel to Maria Austin
1747	June 17, 1823	Charles Goforth to Lavina Grisham
1748	March 29, 1823	Henry Williams to Sally Butry
1749	April 3, 1823	Andrew Watson to Susan Madson
1750	Aug. ___ 1823	John Staples to Sarah McKinney
1751	Dec. 24, 1823	James Staples to Nancy Smith
1752	Feb. 4, 1823	George Brown to Susannah Punkey
1753	March 11, 1823	Thomas Brown to Elizabeth Moyers
1754	July 22, 1823	Thomas Hervey to Levena Leeth
1755	May 10, 1823	Reuben Thomas to Mary Jones
1756	March 19, 1823	Thomas Higdon to Rebecca Cates
1757	Sept. 20, 1823	Uriah Ellis to Rachel Mosier
1758	Nov. 24, 1823	Genl. Geo. Doherty to Sally Randols
1759	Oct. 1, 1823	Mahlon Gilbreath to Polly Campbell
1760	Sept. 15, 1823	Phebe Harris to Elisa Briant
1761	Feb. 11, 1823	James H. Evans to Dorcas Ashmore
1762	Oct. 18, 1823	Isaac Johnson to Nancy Atkins
1763	Jan. 29, 1823	Jesse Dobkins to Casandra Lile
1764	March 19, 1823	James McGhee to Jenny Evans
1765	Dec. 3, 1823	James D. Franklin to Jane Endsley
1766	June 9, 1824	Reuben Churchman to Nancy Mansfield
1767	Dec. 31, 1823	James Donaldson to Parthena Copeland
1768	Dec. 24, 1823	George Moore to Mary Walker
1769	Feb. 2, 1824	Harvey Elweldon to Levina McCuistian
1770	Nov. 25, 1825	Hugh Mills to Elizabeth Fisher (Might be 1824)
1771	Jan. 15, 1824	Wm. Smith to Barbara McKinney
1772	Sept. 1, 1824	Edward Stiff to Manah Burnett
1773	March 16, 1824	Uriah Dodd to Elizabeth Duncan
1774	Aug. 12, 1824	Moses Childress to Nancy King
1775	June 16, 1824	Samuel Evans to Nancy Locke
1776	Oct. 7, 1825	James Frazier to Lydia Ballinger
1777	Dec. 12, 1824	John Peerman to Mary Bell
1778	May 20, 1824	James Pierce to Sarah Jones
1779	Aug. 17, 1824	John Bishop to Silva Cox
1780	Nov. 4, 1824	James Brewer to Sally Green
1781	Oct. 23, 1823	R.J. Baker to Elizabeth Cate
1782	June 9, 1824	Maston Henderson to Elizabeth Cattharp

1783	Feb. 13, 1824	Stephen Johnson to Elizabeth Day
1784	Dec. 23, (12) 1824	David Anderson to Mary Buckner
1785	May 18, (10) 1824	Richard Turner to Elizabeth Ann Pollock
1786	May 6, 1824	Cavalier Homer to Elizabeth Bryan (Horner)
1787	Nov. 9, 1824	Michael Shoaltz to Betsy Ward
1788	Dec. 6, 1824	Charles Gentry to Rhoda Carson
1789	Dec. 20, 1824	Aaron Newman to Sinai Rankin
1790	Dec. 27, 1824	Robert White to Hannah Cliff
1798	May 26, 1824	Enoch Kelly to Susannah Cate
1792	Aug. 23, 1824	Joseph Tally to Sarah Inman
1793	Feb. 15, 1824	Sants Brazelton to Mary Cox
1794	Oct. 5, 1824	Thomas Anderson to Hannah B. Moore
1795	Sept. 1, 1824	James B. Moyers to Cynthia Carson
1796	July 21, 1824	Robert H. Snoddy to Elizabeth Donaldson
1797	Aug. 19, 1824	Thomas Nelson to Charity Gaut
1798	Dec. 11, 1824	Alfred Cartiller to Rhoda Outer
1799	March 4, 1823	Daniel Haney to Narcissa Semrell
1800	Aug. 29, 1824	Henry Stuart to Marjah McConnell
1801	Jan. 26, 1824	Thos. Roddy to Lydia Nenny
1802	July 12, 1824	Solomon Adamson to Sally Summons
1803	Sept. 13, 1824	Thomas Cannon to Lucy Large
1804	Dec. 9, 1823	Thomas Dogget to Lucinda Sampson (probably 1824)
1805	Sept. 26, 1824	Azarah Riggs to Susannah Shepard
1806	July 27, 1824	John R. Eggar to Elizabeth Martin
1814	Nov. 29, 1824	Nicholas Hays to Elizabeth Bare
1815	Sept. 22, 1824	Wm. Rice to Hannah Helton
1816	March 22, 1824	Isaac Day to Martha F. Johnson
1817	Dec. 24, 1824	Samuel Riggs to Elizabeth Chaney
1818	March 2, 1824	James Frazier to Editha Hodges
1819	March 25, 1824	Elijah Mills and Nancy Elmore
1820	Oct. 20, 1824	Robert Jones to Betsy Thornhill
1821	June 2, 1824	Hiram Glass to Sarah Brazelton
1822	Sept. 16, 1824	Russel Milles to Rachel Barnett
1823	Aug. 4, 1824	Jacob Thomas to Mary Callahan
1824	Jan. 19, 1824	John Riggs to Susannah Chapman
1825	July 6, 1824	Nathan Gammon to Mary Hamilton
1826	Dec. 16, 1824	Jacob Johnston to Ershula Glossip
1827	Feb. 7, 1824	Elias Wester to Keziah Boatman
1828	Aug. 13, 1824	Henry Milliken to Elizabeth Geer
1829	Jan. 19, 1824	Wm. Moyers to Margaret Branner
1830	Dec. 6, 1824	Henry Bales to Susannah Hankins
1831	Nov. 25, 1824	Simon Jones to Rebecca Haney
1832	July 24, 1824	James Lane to Ruthie Gossip
1833	Oct. 13, 1824	Elijah Reed to Sally Cox
1834	Dec. 15, 1824	Edward Shipley to Elizabeth Thomas
1835	Nov. 8, 1824	James Hown (Horn) to Fanny Horner
1836	April 27, 1824	Mathas Johnson to Polly Meadows
1837	Jan. 21, 1824	John Darr to Eleanor Dick
1838	March 18, 1850?	(Probably 1824) Oliver Province to Elizabeth Wood

1839	April 20, 1825	Hugh McCall to Jenny Putman
1840	Aug. 4, 1825	Wm. Black to Elizabeth Malcom
1841	June 29, 1825	Isaac Black to Polly Tallant
1842	Feb. 2, 1825	James Sartin to Dorcas Sartin
1843	Nov. 3, 1825	Wm. Lindsy to Martha Pullins
1844	Feb. 16, 1825	Elijah Birch to Nancy Witt
1845	Sept. 15, 1825	Jas. Thomas to Mary Johnson
1846	April 20, 1825	James Bolin to Hannah Bolin
1847	Dec. 5, 1821	Francis Baldridge to Sallie Rodgers
1848	Dec. 20, 1825	James Williams to Rachel Cox
1849	Feb. 26, 1825	Norman Cox to Peggy Hyans (Ryans)
1850	Oct. 7, 1825	Washington Duke to Dorcas Campbell
1851	July 31, 1824	John Janeway to Nancy Sanders
1852	June 11, 1825	Solomon Wolly to Elizabeth Kelsey
1853	Nov. 1, 1825	Wm. McCampbell to Sarah Caldwell
1854	Nov. 24, 1825	David Larrance to Nancy Ballinger
1855	Jan. 29, 1825	Wm. Smith to Lydia Mills
1856	June 1, 1825	Adam Haun to Polly Austin
1857	Nov. 12, 1825	Bradley Eckles to Betsey Peck
1858	Jan. 13, 1825	Daniel Manley to Elizabeth McClanahan
1859	Nov. 1, 1825	Robert J. Wilson to Isabella McFarland
1860	Sept. 16, 1824	Charles Gibbons (?) to Hannah Kelsey
1861	Aug. 22, 1825	Daniel Rach to Catharine Bethel
1862	Jan. 26, 1825	Robertson McCenky to Lydia McDonald
1863	March 2, 1825	Jacob Carwils to Edeline Lane
1864	July 12, 1825	Thomas Love to Eliza Graham
1865	Aug. 23, 1825	Nathan Patterson to Rebecca Newman
1866	Oct. 13, 1825	Enoch Hays to Margaret Canay
1867	June 14, 1825	Walter Bales to Margaret Patton
1868	Feb. 21, 1825	James Cofman to Eliza Robertson
1869	March 12, 1825	Nathaniel Young to Mary Mills
1870	June 23, 1824	(1825) James Brown to Mary White
1871	Jan. 17, 1825	Lewis Nelson to Tabitha Rogers
1872	Sept. 5, 1825	John Davis to Rachel Henderson
1873	Jan. 3, 1825	James Sampson to Sally Geer
1874	May 3, 1825	Geo. W. Clemmons to Rebecca Hurnet
1875	Feb. 1, 1825	James Milliken to Mary Sunderland
1876	May 17, 1825	Robert Martin to Jane Craig
1877	June 29, 1825	John Sterling to Catherine Bare
1878	Aug. 4, 1825	Hiram Loyd to Dotea Flowers
1879	Nov. 16, 1825	Charles Elder to Elizabeth Underwood
1880	Aug. 1, 1825	Ransom Lile to Jane McCuistian
1881	Sept. 20, 1825	Isaac Crow to Annie Jefferies
1882	July 19, 1825	Alex Farmer to Nancy Moser
1883	Dec. 10, 1825	Simmons Bonman to Elizabeth Hill
1884	Dec. 21, 1825	Thomas Adamson to Jane Patton
1885	Jan. 6, 1825	Robert N. Henderson to Winny Endaly
1886	Dec. 13, 1825	James Daniel to Laretia Lively
1887	Nov. 7, 1825	Wm. Cate to Susannah Lock
1888	April 28, 1825	Wm. Conway to Lavina Cannile
1889	Jan. 22, 1825	Latin Moore to Nancy Brooks
1890	Feb. 14, 1825	James Davidson to Nancy Hurt

1891	Jan. 22, 1825	John Walker to Annie Ellis
1892	Oct. 7, 1825	Wm. Helton to Leanna Kiles (might be Lyles)
1893	Dec. 9, 1825	Jesse Gray to E. Moore
1894	Sept. 14, 1825	Francis Young to Polly Smith
1895	July 23, 1825	Charles Palmer to Elizabeth Weaver
1896	July 28, 1825	Wm. Adams to Margaret McNiston
1897	Nov. 18, 1825	David Shepherd to Matilda Williams
1898	Sept. 8, 1825	Washington Rippetoe to Elizabeth Reams
1899	Sept. 15, 1825	Jacob Cline to Elizabeth Cline
1900	Nov. 7, 1825	Isaac Lock to Mary Cates
1901	April 18, 1825	Dennis Gibson to Priscilla Parrott
1902	May 17, 1825	Jesse Taff to Jane Davis
1903	Aug. 24, 1825	John Watkins to Mary Cox
1904	Jan. 29, 1825	John Sartin to Caty Critches
1905	May 5, 1825	Hugh Canhorn to Rebecca Callahan
1906	May 23, 1825	David Grant to Elizabeth McDonald
1907	Feb. 19, 1825	Abner Hillett to Fanny Rippetoe
1908	April 5, 1825	Robert Hamilton to Jane Martin
1909	Feb. 24, 1825	Geo. W. Pulse to Margaret Keeney
1910	Oct. 22, 1825	Benj. J. Wilson to Betsey Dick
1911	March 8, 1825	James Bailey to Rebecca Manner
1912	Feb. 3, 1825	Simon Patterson to Sarah Newman
1913	March 2, 1825	John Douglas to Margaret Underwood
1914	Dec. 8, 1825	Robt. Shubert to Lydia Reynolds
1915	Nov. 8, 1825	James Wise to Catherine Stephenson
1916	Aug. 16, 1825	Martin B. Coiles to Eliza Brazelton
1917	March 8, 1825	John Chambers to Anny Edmunds
1918	Jan. 29, 1825	Jas. Baker to Elizabeth Taff
1919	Feb. 3, 1825	Wm. Franklin to Mary Ann Pankey
1920	Feb. 3, 1825	Robert Vance to Abagail Jones
1921	Nov. 28, 1825	John D. Snoddy to Jene McDonald
1922	_____, 1825	Steny Minger to Mary Ketner
1923	March 8, 1825	Morgan Maples to Sarah Murphy
1924	Nov. 23, 1825	Thomas Seal to Catherine Hutchinson
1925	Dec. 19, 1825	Andrew Walker to Polly Lane
1926	Nov. 13, 1825	Samuel Rankin to Margaret Phillips
1927	Feb. , 1825	Richard D. Reems to Mary Stoples
1928	Nov. 19, 1825	Richard Thornhill to Margaret Cline
1929	Nov. 20, 1825	Archibald Austin to Mary Dogget
1930	Aug. 14, 1826	Philip Eslinger to Phebe Black
1931	Feb. 1, 1827	Wm. H. Miller to Ann Miller
1932	Aug. 8, 1826	Geo. D. Edgar to Eliza D. Morrow
1933	Oct. 18, 1827	Wm. Faust to Deborah Hankins
1934	April 6, 1826	Benj. Neal to Patsy Elmore
1935	June 15, 1826	John G. Jones to Nancy Walton
1936	Nov. 18, 1826	John Minick to Rebecca Chatman
1937	Aug. 5, 1826	Zebedel Wills to Jane Kelly

1938	Dec. 26, 1826	Mathews Johnson to Peggy Quarrles
1939	July 26, 1826	Elijah Moore to Caroline Parks
1940	Sept. 8, 1826	Wm. McNice to Ann Coppock
1941	Nov. 16, 1826	John Peck to Polly Manley
1942	Sept. 7, 1826	Charles Cates to Rachel Thornburgh
1943	March 23, 1827	James Williams to Mary Cox
1944	March 27, 1827	Wm. Sellers to Pheba Thornburgh
1945	Sept. 13, 1826	John Ellis to Elizabeth A. White
1946	July 4, 1826	Robert H. Hynds to Mary Jane W. Moore
1947	Jan. 2, 1827	John McClister to Ester Day
1948	June 12, 1827	Alfred Hagans to Jane Routh
1949	Aug. 16, 1827	Robert McDonald to Betsy Ann King
1950	Oct. 29, 1827	W. Summers to Hannah Mills
1951	March 4, 1826	Solomon Ruth to Sarah Dood
1952	Sept. 11, 1826	Alex Blackburn to Priscilla Morrow
1953	Nov. 22, 1826	George A. Myers to Catherine Nichalson
1954	Nov. 11, 1826	Wm. McClister to Jerusha Foster
1955	Oct. 10, 1826	Thomas Stringfield to Sarah Williams
1956	June 12, 1826	Geo. W. Drake to Mary Gentry
1957	July 17, 1826	John Frank to H. M. Woods
1958	Aug. 8, 1826	Jesse Cooper to Elizabeth Huston
1959	April 7, 1826	Thomas Cate to Rebecca Lawrence
1960	Feb. 15, 1826	Patton Howel to Nancy Ruth
1961	March 12, 1826	Jefferson Woods to Amanda Snodgrass
1962	April 16, 1826	James Bottom to Sarah Carr
1963	May 22, 1827	Thomas Housley to Eliza Hodges
1964	April 17, 1827	James Crow to Rosana Chaney
1965	Sept. 11, 1827	Lewis Christman to Mary G. Nenney
1966	Jan. 14, 1827	James Candike to Sarah Hoggatt
1967	May 19, 1826	Henry Chambers to Sarah Keeney
1968	Nov. 20, 1826	Presley W. Fraser to Sarah Benyan
1969	Oct. 22, 1827	Robert Housley to Lucinda Childres
1970	June 30, 1827	Jesse Douglas to Polly Douglas
1971	Nov. 6, 1827	James Hill to Betsy Black
1972	Oct. 25, 1827	Thomas Sellers to Nancy Bales
1973	Sept. 13, 1827	Henry Turner to Anny Cate
1974	Oct. 18, 1827	Jacob Sherrock to Rebecca Letter
1975	July 26, 1827	John G. W. Rice to Lavina Jane Smith
1976	Oct. 24, 1827	Jonathan Lawrence to Anna Woodward
1977	April 9, 1827	Wm. R. Copeland to Lavina Jacks
1978	Feb. 7, 1827	Nathan Hillion to Eliza Ritter
1979	Sept. 6, 1827	Thomas Vanhooser to Polly Bales
1980	Aug. 29, 1827	Mathew Childress to Martha King
1981	June 9, 1826	Wm. Branson (Branon) to Rebecca Kimbrough
1982	Nov. 2, 1826	Henry Frey to Elizabeth Peck
1983	March 14, 1827	John Sellers to Patsey Hodge

41

1984	April 25, 1827	Thomas McGuire to Rechal Ashmore
1985	Oct. 16, 1827	John McDonald to Nancy Snoddy
1986	May 29, 1827	John Macy to Alice Mills
1987	Feb. 14, 1827	John Phillips to Elizabeth Cluck
1988	May 21, 1827	Robert Patton to Nancy Martin
1989	March 15, 1827	Samuel Lewis to Lucinda Henshaw
1990	Aug. 18, 1827	Lewis McDaniel to Nancy Lewis (no return)
1991	Aug. 23, 1827	Wm. Edwards to Rachel Macy
1992	Feb. 26, 1827	Zachariah Shields to Catherine Bainwater
1993	Jan. 16, 1827	Jonathan Wood to Margaret H. Inman
1994	Dec. 24, 1827	Wm. Rian to Elizabeth Cline
1995	April 27, 1827	John G. Crump to Eliza G. Watkins
1996	Feb. 21, 1827	Jonathan Routh to Catherine Baringer
1997	July 11, 1827	Daniel Reams to Nancy Holdaway
1998	March 22, 1827	Jacob Golden to Alice Frazer
1999	March 7, 1827	Richard Night to Rebecca Weeden
2000	April 17, 1827	Joseph M. Fergison to Catherine Miller
2001	Feb. 19, 1827	Benjamine A. Blackburn to Isabel M. Caldwell
2002	Dec. 11, 1826	Pleasant Hammock and M. Murphy
2003	Feb. 21, 1826	Edward T. Jett to Malinda Mansfield
2004	Jan. 6, 1826	John Elmore to Joanna Douglas
2005	Feb. 11, 1826	Jesse Deskins to Elizabeth Hill
2006	Dec. 19, 1826	Peter North to Sally Copeland
2007	July 1, 1826	Jeremiah Walker to Nancy McGlowan
2008	March 1, 1826	Wm. Templeton to Sophia W. Newton
2009	June 7, 1826	Joseph Hooker to Rebecca Myrick
2010	Jan. 21, 1826	John W. Boyd to Leanah Cox
2011	Nov. 14, 1826	Wm. Shannon to Mary McBrown
2012	Feb. 21, 1826	Jacob Frizzell to Elizabeth Lane
2013	May 7, 1826	James Pangle to Eda Lane
2014	May 22, 1827	Joseph I. Farris to Jane Rogers
2015	April 2, 1827	Jonathan Ketner to Sarah Smelser
2016	March 7, 1827	Elijah Hill to Elizabeth Darr
2017	Dec. 24, 1827	John H. Keener to Elizabeth Sasseen
2018	Jan. 24, 1827	Martin Denton and Parthena Cofman
2019	March 7, 1827	Thomas Night to Mary Dunn
2020	Feb. 22, 1827	Wm. Carmichael to Sarah Ann Gann
2021	July 22, 1827	James Taylor to Sally Davis
2022	June 27, 1827	Wm. Shannon to Mary Ann McCuistian
2023	June 9, 1827	Wm. Maze to Elizabeth Jacob
2024	Aug. 18, 1827	Robert C. Mills to Rebecca Cate
2025	Aug. 15, 1827	Joseph Jolly to Rebecca Thornton
2026	March 29, 1827	John Dickey to Rebecca Kedner
2027	Dec. 11, 1827	Wm. Adcock to Sarah O. Howell
2028	Feb. 15, 1827	Isaac Brazelton to Mary Frazer

JEFFERSON COUNTY MARRIAGES

2029	Feb. 19, 1827	Martin Henson to Rachel Baninger (?)
2030	Jan. 23, 1826	Geo. Buly to Mahala Cuder
2031	Sept. 11, 1827	Shadrick Manard to Marjah Hall
2032	June 26, 1827	Benony Kimbrough to Peggy Givens
2033	March 6, 1827	Pleasant Bales to Elizabeth Hamlet
2034	Nov. 29, 1827	Martin O. Atchley and Frankey Carman
2035	Aug. 20, 1827	Peter Russell to Elizabeth Felknor
2036	June 21, 1827	Geo. Pierce to Martha Burnett
2037	May 13, 1826	Reps Jones to Delila Harrison
2038	March 3, 1827	John Callahan to Celia Bailey
2039	Feb. 2, 1827	John Line to Juda Walter
2040	Aug. 15, 1827	Wm. McDaniel to Margaret Eller
2041	May 7, 1826	Joseph Janeway to Mary Smith
2042	July 16, 1827	Royal Turner to Margaret Pollock
2043	Feb. 8, 1827	Vaden Perrin to Sarah Churchman
2044	May 22, 1827	Thomas Daniel to Catherine Dalton
2045	Aug. 9, 1827	James Turner to Phebe Maples
2046	May 2, 1827	Thomas Day to Polly Copeland
2047	July 14, 1827	Joshua Jones to Margaret Dick
2048	March 4, 1826	Benjamine Janeway to Margaret McGoys
2049	Aug. 31, 1826	John Rogers to Elender Campbell
2050	Oct. 14, 1826	James Woods to Martha Harris
2051	May 28, 1826	Robert Bales to Polly McCleany
2052	Aug. 21, 1826	Robert Kelly to Rebecca Elder
2053	June 14, 1826	Wm. T. Morrow to Lauvina Jarnagin
2054	Aug. 7, 1827	Edward Francis to Margaret Winters
2055	Dec. 20, 1827	Samuel Surrate to Polly Oldhance
2056	Feb. 9, 1827	Geo. Miller to Jean Martin
2057	Sept. 23, 1827	Wm. Abbott to Sally Frisbee
2058	Jan. 27, 1825/7	Ebenezer Leeth to Polly Larrance
2059	April 5, 1827	Peter Ruble to James Shelly
2060	April 24, 1827	Wm. Slaton to Matilda Sampson
2061	Oct. 1, 1827	John Blackburn to Christiana Branner
2062	Nov. 6, 1827	Christopher Williams to Elizabeth Brittner
2063	Aug. 19, 1827	David Haworth to Susannah Bales
2064	June 20, 1826	Wm. S. King to Hester Cox
2065	Aug. 10, 1826	Samuel Willes to Elizabeth Morris
2066	Nov. 10, 1827	Robert Burchfield to Anne Malcourt
2067	Aug. 2, 1826	David Campbell to Cassa Carwile
2068	Sept. 2, 1827	John Rinehart to Abagail Hill
2069	Jan. 11, 1827	Obadiah Penketon to Easler Kimbrough
2070	April 22, 1826	Isaac B. Cannon to Jane W. Palmer
2071	April 18, 1826	Abner Jolly to Betsey Hammond
2072	Feb. 13, 1826	Jesse Phelan to Dice Neal
2073	Jan. 26, 1826	John Cox to Caster Evans
2074	Feb. 15, 1826	Anthony Caldwell to Polly V. McSpadden

2075	Oct. 19, 1826	Nathan David to Betsy Cox
2076	Oct. 11, 1826	Henry Shields to Jane Dick
2077	Nov. 27, 1827	Isaac M. Newman to Sally Underwood
2078	Oct. 26, 1828	Calloway Hodge to Betsey Braden
2079	Jan. 22, 1828	James G. Newman to Elizabeth Harman
2080	June 19, 1828	Edward Newman to Nancy Medlow
2081	Jan. 12, 1828	Ezekiel Goan to Leannah McClannahan
2082	Feb. 9, 1828	John Cofman to Elizabeth Witt
2083	Feb. 15, 1828	James Rugh to Patsy King
2084	Aug. 5, 1828	Wm. Hanson to Mary Inman
2085	Oct. 14, 1828	Samuel McAdro to Elizabeth Pigg
2086	April 19, 1828	Solomon Mills to Polly Headly
2087	Jan. 23, 1828	James H. Carson to Lavina T. Carson
2088	May 15, 1828	John Mills to Polly Janeway
2089	May 29, 1828	Bradley Kimbrough to Margaret Pankey
2090	July 2, 1828	Preston J. Johnson to Mary Jones
2091	March 7, 1828	Abraham Lowe to Carolina M. H. Morrow
2092	Sept. 4, 1828	Napoleon B. Bradford to Emly G. Reese
2093	Sept. 4, 1828	John Moore to Vicey Cockram (no return)
2094	Oct. 14, 1828	Abram Keeney to Rosana Blackburn
2095	April 22, 1828	Isaac Renean to Melissa Newman
2096	March 24, 1828	Washington Boling to Julia Ann Boles
2097	Aug. 12, 1828	Isaac A. Miller to Susan Swann
2098	Jan. 22, 1828	Benjamine McCormick to Elizabeth Davis
2099	Jan. 26, 1828	Hezekiah Tague to Jane Hamlet
2100	Jan. 14, 1828	Wm. Mewman to Catharine Hammon
2101	Nov. 10, 1828	Wm. Thornburgh to Rosahah Routh
2102	Aug. 26, 1828	Jeremich Gasiton to Jane McCullah
2103	Sept. 15, 1828	M. H. McSpadden to Sarah Henry
2104	April 30, 1828	Jas. O. Howell to Sarah Cox
2105	Jan. 28, 1828	Preston Stinett to Elizabeth Bryan
2106	April 2, 1828	Jesse Baley to Polly Gliffer
2107	Feb. 19, 1828	Henry Stamith to Elizabeth Jarnegan (Smith)
2108	June 5, 1828	Wm. Baker to Jane Estis
2109	Sept. 16, 1828	Jethro Hill to Mary Cate
2110	March 25, 1828	Jesse Riggs to Celia Chelton
2111	Dec. 15, 1828	John Robinson to Mary Holdway
2112	July 23, 1828	Lewellan Rice to M. Former (no return)
2113	Dec. 15, 1828	Levi Voils to Lucy lasent
2114	Oct. 15, 1828	Amos Monos to Elizabeth Francis
2115	Aug. 14, 1828	Jesse Young to Mariah Maston
2116	Aug. 7, 1828	Geo. Henderson to Lucy Bacholar
2117	March 26, 1828	Allen McDaniels to Hannah Galoway

2118	March 8, 1828	Wm. McAndrew to Polly Denton
2119	Dec. 12, 1828	Gaslong Williams to Mary Welsh
2120	July 7, 1828	John Roberson to Susan Riddle
2121	Feb. 9, 1828	John S. Witt to Mary Imman
2122	April 13, 1828	Jas. McDanil to Eliza Ann Reed
2123	Nov. 13, 1828	Samil Baker to Florence Rhea
2124	Nov. 29, 1828	Wm. Witt to Elizabeth Maze
2125	Aug. 23, 1828	Isaac Alderson to Susannah Coppock
2126	Nov. 13, 1828	Elijah Sampson to Marry Phillips
2127	Oct. 28, 1828	John Joey to Jane Churchman
2128	Aug. 20, 1828	Robt. D. Franklin to Jane Cannon
2129	July 23, 1828	Joab. Tsevillion to Elizabeth Franklin
2130	Nov. 3, 1828	James Hickman to Chaney Hann
2131	Dec. 2, 1828	Thos. S. Clevenger to Sarah Kimbrough
2132	Aug. 14, 1828	Wm. Castwright to Mary Brake
2133	Aug. 12, 1828	James Anderson to Elizabeth Sartion (no return)
2134	Nov. 24, 1828	Minnard Thornburgh to Sarah Rankin
2135	Dec. 27, 1828	Alex Helton to Nancy Boatman
2136	Aug. 12, 1828	Daniel Manard. to Mulbury Franklin
2137	Feb. 28, 1828	Pleasant Pankey to Elizabeth Massengill
2138	Jan. 28, 1828	Ezekile E. Smith to Betsy Boiley
2139	Dec. 11, 1828	Wyley Duke to Elizabeth Pasker
2140	Jan. 5, 1828	John G. Duke to Bessey Farmner
2141	July 30, 1828	Joel Elmore to Susanah Fielden
2142	Dec. 24, 1828	Job Dee to Margaret Caster
2143	Feb. 25, 1828	Needham Jarnagin to Margaret Nanney
2144	June 28, 1828	Robt. Bales to Lucinda Russell
2145	March 1, 1828	Isaac Doggett to Susanah McCurne
2146	Dec. 2, 1828	Joseph Shedden to Elizabeth Richey
2147	April 5, 1828	Andrew McComick to Jane Franklin
2148	Nov. 15, 1828	Bryant Burrows to Polly Ann Walker
2149	Oct. 7, 1828	Benj. F. McFarland to Malinda Harle
2150	April 23, 1828	Isaac Davidson to Hepsey Douglass
2151	Nov. 27, 1828	Daniel Walker to Harriet Bunis
2152	Dec. 22, 1828	John A. Smith to Martha M. Rea
2153	Dec. 9, 1828	Thomas Carback to Emaline Edgar
2154	Sept. 10, 1828	David Williams to T. Sartin
2155	July 16, 1828	Willis Rippetoe to Catherine Conner
2156	Oct. 28, 1828	James Fielden to Elizabeth Smidden (no return)
2157	Dec. 15, 1828	John Robeson to Mary Holdaway (no return)
2158	Feb. 15, 1828	Hugh M. Elder to Margaret Denton
2159	Feb. 23, 1828	James Reppetoe to Hannah Evans

2160	July 3, 1828	Stephen W. Hodge to Mary E. Campbell
2161	March 6, 1828	John Squires to Eliza Thornton
2162	Dec. 11, 1828	Ephrain Kitchen to Elizabeth Lockhart
2163	May 13, 1828	Palmer Jack to Jane Irwin
2164	June 9, 1828	Andrew B. Edgar to Sarah Baldridge
2165	Nov. 8, 1828	Andrew C. Patton to Nancy Jane Lane
2166	July 27, 1828	Joe Gregory to Martha Peasland
2167	Dec. 9, 1828	Thomas Carback to Emaline Edgar
2168	Sept. 10, 1828	David Williams to T. Sartin
2169	July 16, 1828	Willis Rippetoe to Catharine Conner
2170	Oct. 28, 1828	James Fielden to Elizabeth Smidden
2171	Dec. 15, 1828	John Robinson to Mary Holdaway (no return)
2172	Feb. 15, 1828	Hugh M. Elder to Margaret Denton
2173	Feb. 23, 1828	James Rippetoe to Hannah Evans
2174	July 3, 1828	Stephen W. Hodge to Mary E. Campbell
2175	March 5, 1828	John Squires to Eliza Thornton
2176	Dec. 11, 1828	Ephrain Kitchen to Elizabeth Lockhart
2177	May 13, 1829	Palmer Jack to Jane Irvin
2178	June 8, 1829	Andrew B. Edgar to Sarah Baldridge
2179	Nov. 8, 1829	Andrew C. Patton to Nancy Jane Lane
2180	July 27, 1829	Joe Gregory to Martha Peasland
2181	Jan. 25, 1829	J. Hickman to Mary Bales
2182	May 30, 1829	Em. Locke to Mary Nitchell
2183	Dec. 20, 1829	Wm. Caldwell to Cordilla Blackburn
2184	May 25, 1829	Samuel Thompson to Mary McClannaban
2185	Aug. 15, 1829	Hyran Trustly to Martha McKinney
2186	Oct. 5, 1829	Wm. Danaldson to Martha Reynold
2187	Sept. 15, 1829	Thomas B. Jarmagin to Eliza Donaldson
2188	Oct. 16, 1829	Wyle H. Adans to Lucinda Gregory
2189	Aug. 3, 1829	James Frank to Elizabeth Woods
2190	Feb. 10, 1829	Wm. Forrester to Catharine Flknor
2191	Dec. 28, 1829	John Mills to Elizabeth Manly
2192	Jan. 27, 1829	Washington Thompson to Ruthey French
2193	Sept. 3, 1829	Isaac H. Wilson to Martha Bates
2194	Sept. 14, 1829	Silas Henry to Ester McSpadden
2195	Sept. 11, 1829	Andrew Douglass to Mary Adamson
2196	Sept. 9, 1829	Josiah Fain to Mehala W. Denton
2197	Nov. 10, 1829	Edward V. Barnett to Nancy Stiff
2198	April 22, 1829	Francis Puckett to Nancy Gibson
2199	March 20, 1829	Henry Bales to L. Summers
2200	Dec. 21, 1829	Bennitt Allen to Louise Doggett
2201	July 20, 1829	Mordecai Elmore to Elizabeth Randolph

2202	Aug. 11, 1829	John Pogne to Patsy Hannonds
2203	Dec. 14, 1829	James H. Gass to Malinda Blackburn
2204	Jan. 7, 1829	Wm. Day to Levicy McKee
2205	Nov. 10, 1829	Henry Parks to Susan Gregory
2206	Nov. 28, 1829	Wm. Combs to Jane Bearman
2207	Dec. 25, 1829	Obed C. Thornburgh to Priscilla Mills
2208	Dec. 26, 1829	Martin H. Gibson to Margaret Newman
2209	Jan. 15, 1829	John Chowel to Catherine Patton
2210	Feb. 26, 1829	John Miller to Polly Moore
2211	Aug. 13, 1829	Lewis Martin, Sr. to Mary Ann Pope
2212	March 7, 1829	Joel W. Denneston to Margaret Denniston
2213	July 23, 1829	Joseph Herron to Elenor Adamson
2214	July 4, 1829	Stephen Scarlett to Mary Cates
2215	March 5, 1829	Alexander Douglass to Mary Cheldup
2216	April 8, 1829	James Pollard to Susan Bowls
2217	March 7, 1829	D. Mullins to Nancy Polak (no return)
2218	Dec. 15, 1829	Harvey Riggs to Rachel McKinney
2219	Aug. 13, 1829	Pleasant Snow to Fanny McKinney
2220	Aug. 29, 1829	David Coward to Mary Ann Hazlewood
2221	Oct. 20, 1829	Josiah Mills to Elizabeth M. Hutchson
2222	March 8, 1829	Thomas Smith to Dolly A. Cox (no return)
2223	May 31, 1829	Robert Deniston to Polly Perrion
2224	July 30, 1829	James Welch to Elenor Bailey
2225	Aug. 15, 1829	Samuel Cates to Vena Summers
2226	Sept. 19, 1829	David Gwinn to Elizabeth Carr
2227	July 25, 1829	David Wright to Margaret Quarrells
2228	Sept. 1, 1829	James Burnett to Sarah O. Buant
2229	Aug. 9, 1829	Zachary Tollaver to Darah Hickman
2230	___ 25, 1829	Peter Benton to Martha Wilhite
2231	May 4, 1829	Thomas C. Rankin to Elvira Blackburn
2232	Jan. 27, 1829	Wiley Line to Nancy Kidwell
2233	Jan. 1. 1829	Wm. Griffin to Mary King
2234	Oct. 18, 1829	Thomas Carmichael to Nancy Walker
2235	Jan. 15, 1829	John Gideons to Polly Evans
2236	Nov. 21, 1829	Thomas A. Hoskins to Nancy Riley
2237	Dec. 29, 1829	Joseph Burchfiel to Rachel H. Russell
2238	March 25, 1829	Moses B. Milles to Keziah Harris
2239	Aug. 27, 1829	Baxter Thompson to Rachel Brown
2240	Oct. 31, 1829	Samuel Williams to Charity West
2241	Feb. 17, 1829	Hudson Amonett to Mary Carmichael
2242	Sept. 3, 1829	Jesse Roberson to Anne Doggett
2243	Feb. 14, 1829	James Smith to Vetsey Hickey
2244	Oct. 28, 1829	Thomas Cocke to Harriet Harle
2245	Aug. 26, 1829	Daniel D. Noland to Mary McDaniel

```
2246  July 13, 1829    James Dangston to L. Davis
2247  Sept. 7, 1829    Abel Chancy to Eda Millikan
2248  Feb. 25, 1829    Wm. Barnett to Elizabeth Treadway
2249  Dec. 25, 1829    Jacob Walker to Dusty Curry
2250  Oct. 29, 1829    Samuel Cofman to Sophia Coltharp
2251  Dec. 20, 1829    Robert Noore to Elizabeth Walker
                        (no return)
2252  March 2, 1829    Bejamine Gaut to Matilda Nicholas
2253  June 1, 1829     Thomas Neas to Nancy Cox
2254  Feb. 10, 1829    Wesley Smith to Nancy Davis
2255  Dec. 7, 1829     Josiah Young to Sally Dickins
2256  Nov. 7, 1829     Phelik Tyler to Hohanna Riddle
2257  May 7, 1829      Nelson Ivey to Ruth Davis (May)
2258  Sept. 21, 1829   Arthur Long to Delana Royl
2259  Feb. 17, 1829    Geo. Campbell to Elenor Monut
2260  Jan. 13, 1829    Wm. Kelly to Patsy Walker
2261  May 3, 1829      Josiah Frisbee to Amenca Eastep
2262  Sept. 29, 1829   Andrew J. Margreves to Rhoda C.
                        Rogers
2263  Dec. 8, 1828     Manning Summers to Mahala Underwood
2264  Aug. 18, 1830    Simon French to Gulda Lyles
2265  Jan. 29, 1830    Adam H. McBee to Mariah L. Donlds
2266  Dec. 15, 1830    Thomas Givens to Susanah Kitchen
2267  May 14, 1830     Wesley Stubblefield to Matilda
                        Milikan
2268  Jan. 13, 1830    John Routh to Sarah Baton
2269  Oct. 25, 1830    Anthony Caldwill to Martha K.
                        McSpadden
2270  April 14, 1830   Jas A. Harris to Harriet P. Parrott
2271  Jan. 29, 1830    Thomas A. McSpadden to Susan
                        Epnght
2272  May 18, 1830     John M. Bruce to Nancy McClannahan
2273  Feb. 11, 1830    Calvin Bales to Elizabeth Coppick
2274  Dec. 29, 1830    Lafford French to Mary Kimbrough
2275  May 6, 1830      Wm. Henshay to Matilda Done
2276  Nov. 6, 1830     Leander Lee to Martha Maples
2277  March 18, 1830   Sampson Cox to Elizabeth Driskell
2278  Aug. 18, 1830    Wm. McKee to Matilda Lanksle
2279  Nov. 16, 1830    Thomas K. Coffman to Nancy Parmer
2280  July 17, 1830    Jas. McMarland to Vinie Wilson
2281  Feb. 25, 1830    Wm. Gist to Sarah Tyler
2282  Sept. 15, 1830   Eli Jones to Eleanor Moore
2283  Dec. 5, 1830     John B. Wilkerson to Elizabeth El
                        Lyles
2284  Nov. 4, 1830     Barnaby King to Charlotte Kelly
2285  Nov. 3, 1830     Stephen Pollard to Mary Mount
2286  Nov. 13, 1830    Jesse Maples to Jane Bowlin
2287  June 12, 1830    Allen Heathcocke to Fannie Adams
2288  June 26, 1830    Wm. Casey to Vine Curry
2289  Feb. 3, 1830     John Carr to Winney Jones
2290  Dec. 8, 1830     Thomas Pollard to Sarah Nount
2291  Jan. 2, 1830     Jeremiah M. Leath to Jane Cass
2292  Oct. 27, 1830    Alex Hau. to Elizabeth Riddle
2293  Aug. 28, 1830    Wm. Cate to Mary Thornourgh
```

2294	Aug. 31, 1830	Obadiah Ward to Nancy Woods
2295	Sept. 4, 1830	Henry Ivey to Eliza Davis
2296	Dec. 15, 1830	Abrahan Thomas to Martha Heath
2297	Sept. 9, 1830	John Drinnen to Elizabeth Mills
2298	Aug. 28, 1830	Charles Campbell to Mary Stone
2299	Dec. 9, 1830	Wm. B. Cunningham to Eliza S. Peck
2300	Feb. 6, 1830	Amos Wilson to Jenny Boem
2301	Feb. 4, 1830	Richard McAndrew to Sarah Ann Gregory
2302	Aug. 22, 1830	John T. Trevillion to Betsey Gilliland
2303	March 9, 1830	Berry Bradson to Patsy McCloud
2304	April 6, 1830	James Carman to Nancy Sage (no return)
2305	July 19, 1830	Adam Large to Nancy Brice
2306	July 23, 1830	Austin Bethel to Lavina Traglen
2307	Nov. 17, 1830	John H. Peck to Sarah Goforth
2308	Jan. 13, 1830	Joel R. Denton to Mary H. Craig
2309	Dec. 29, 1830	Wm. Whalen to Polly Wilson
2310	March 9, 1830	Thomas Gallahan to Rebecca Whillock
2311	Dec. 23, 1830	Joseph Witt to Cynthia Larrance
2312	Dec. 23, 1830	Danile Hearn to Mary Ann Alderson
2313	Oct. 28, 1830	Edmond Chanbres to Mary Bruce
2314	Nov. 25, 1830	John Cass to Dela Lively
2315	May 19, 1830	Robert King to Margaret Haynes
2316	Oct. 12, 1830	John Harnson to Mary Turner
2317	May 22, 1830	Thomas D. Johnson to Thursey White
2318	Dec. 8, 1830	Henry Holston to Manah L. S. Peck
2319	Feb. 18, 1830	Cyms Hays to Anne Ferrell
2320	March 4, 1830	Wm. Black to Jane Miller
2321	April 8, 1830	Wm. P. Carter to Jane Gass
2322	Feb. 24, 1830	Thoedrick Coran to Cooky Annis (no return)
2323	March 20, 1830	James Davis to Anne Love
2324	Nov. 9, 1830	Osborne R. Walker to Adline M. McFarland
2325	Dec. 18, 1830	Elijah Baker to Mary Henderson
2326	Oct. 28, 1830	Geo. Lewis Susanah Spice
2327	Aug. 31, 1830	Thomas Nelson to Sarah Hamlet (no return)
2328	Oct. 12, 1830	Henry McCray to Malinda Taylor
2329	Aug. 31, 1830	Joseph Thornhill to Mary Cass
2330	Nov. 17, 1830	Peter Carwile to Sabra Brimer
2331	Dec. 21, 1830	Right Lane to Margaret Ann Evans
2332	Jan. 7, 1830	Jeriah Leith to Jane Hill
2333	March 8, 1830	Samil Caldwell to Sally Blackburn
2334	March 22, 1830	H. Dougald M. Cate to Mary Ann Adeneal
2335	March 15, 1830	Turner Sharp to Eliza Burkett
2336	Jan. 27, 1830	Wallace McClure to Natilda Fanner
2337	Feb. 27, 1830	Sterling Hodgen to Mary Collins

2338	Oct. 20, 1830	James T. Doherty to Elizabeth Gentry
2339	Jan. 20, 1830	Wilson Naples to Polly Brown
2340	April 13, 1830	Hannibal Donaldson to Eleanor Odeneal
2341	July 27, 1830	John Haun to Perine Brittain
2342	Aug. 12, 1830	H. Noun to Rebecca Patton
2343	Jan. 26, 1832	James Witt to Mary Johnson
2344	April 4, 1831	John Jacob to Lydia McGuire
2345	Oct. 3, 1831	David Caldwell to Mary Blackburn
2346	June 6, 1831	Henry Givens to Anne L. Thornhill
2347	Jan. 18, 1831	Willis James Bradley to Sally Walker
2348	Jan. 11, 1831	J. Watts to Caty Jones
2349	Feb. 28, 1831	John N. Blackburn to Martha Jane C. Morrow
2350	Dec. 5, 1831	John Glossip to Permelia Cunningham
2351	April 3, 1832	William Mays to Eveline Gentry
2352	Dec. 17, 1831	McCryer Bennett to Nancy Foster
2353	April 5, 1831	Leroy Gibson to Elizabeth Phillips
2354	Feb. 12, 1831	William Smith to Patsy Randolph
2355	Jan. 16, 1831	Wm. Gwinn to Lidia Mills
2356	July 20, 1831	Thomas Patton to Susanah Carney
2357	March 7, 1831	Thomas Douglass to Elizabeth Newman
2358	Oct. 5, 1831	Geo. W. Drake to Mary Carson
2359	Aug. 4, 1831	Peter North to Mary Ferrgerson
2360	Oct. 5, 1831	John Lock to Mary Miller
2361	Dec. 31, 1831	Richard Hale to Margaret Myers (no return)
2362	June 18, 1831	Wm. Blair to Elizabeth Taff
2363	Sept. 10, 1831	John Sellers to Sarah Barnes
2364	Dec. 27, 1832	James Marine to Q. Wilcocke
2365	Dec. 1, 1832	Stephen Jerry to Jane Meadows
2366	Dec. 22, 1832	Wm. French to Sally Franklin
2367	Feb. 8, 1832	Joseph Carny to Sarah H. Yates
2368	Nov. 3, 1832	Samuel Hammonds to Jane Grace
2369	Aug. 13, 1832	Thomas Barley to Pelina Franklin
2370	Feb. 20, 1832	John Williams to Melinda McDaniel
2371	Oct. 10, 1832	John Grant to Elenor Carter
2372	Jan. 23, 1832	Joseph D. Hodges to Francis Hodges
2373	May 28, 1832	Jowell Heath to Unice Thomas
2374	July 23, 1832	James Hoskins to Aloy Davis
2375	March 19, 1832	Nelson Ore to Ann Smith
2376	Jan. 19, 1832	Robert D. Franklin to Mary McDannel
2377	Dec. 18, 1832	Wm. H. Moffett to Nancy M. Gillespie
2378	June 20, 1832	Albert Pierce to Mahala Davis
2379	July 10, 1832	Wm. Wright to Rutha Scheckels
2380	Sept. 17, 1832	John P. Mathews to Jane A. Rankin
2381	Sept. 4, 1832	Martin Gentry to Betsy Rinehart

2382	Aug. 20, 1832	Martin Bunch to Elizabeth Hance
2383	Dec. 26, 1832	James Cox to Nancy Worley
2384	Aug. 20, 1832	James Wilson to Elizabeth Lyle
2385	Aug. 4, 1832	Jo. Mathew Gaut to Delila Thompson
2386	Feb. 11, 1832	Thomas Kimbrough to Elizabeth Austell
2387	July 7, 1832	Abram Smith to Elizabeth Hadley (no return)
2388	Jan. 2, 1832	Henry E. Massengill to Mary E. Patton
2389	Sept. 26, 1832	Thomas F. Mills to Manerva Brownlow
2390	Oct. 5, 1832	Samuel Petty to Dorothy Shelly
2391	Nov. 29, 1832	John V. Haynes to Sarah J. Wormsley
2392	Sept. 12, 1832	Lacy Kimbrough to Betsey Jones
2393	Jan. 11, 1832	James Ramsey to Eleanor Ramsey
2394	Aug. 5, 1832	George Coffman to Jane Welsh
2395	Oct. 17, 1832	Willie Mitchell to Mary Ann Love
2396	Nov. 14, 1832	Pleasant S. Churchman to Mary Shelly
2397	Dec. 29, 1832	Isaac A. Menson to Rachel Tanner
2398	Dec. 12, 1832	Preston Underwood to Casander Doherty
2399	Nov. 21, 1832	Henry Randolph to Susan D. Kimbrough
2400	Aug. 4, 1832	James Hudson to Elizabeth Manley
2401	Jan. 19, 1831	Gideon L. Brown to Matilda Patton
2402	May 29, 1832	Stephen Large to Mary Dodd
2403	Jan. 25, 1832	R. F. Campbell to Jane David (Davis)
2404	Jan. 5, 1832	Robert C. Mills to Martha Duncan
2405	March 29, 1832	John Newman to Sarah Darr
2406	March 26, 1832	Thomas Davis to Lavina Hill
2407	Feb. 8, 1832	Isaac Purkpile to Elizabeth McKee
2408	March 5, 1832	George Graham to Eliza Ann Graham
2409	April 26, 1832	Levi Smith to Elizabeth Newman
2410	Dec. 15, 1832	Wm. Abbott to D. Brittain
2411	April 27, 1832	Samuel C. Davidson to Isabella McClannahan
2412	May 16, 1832	James Coffman to Betsey Carr
2413	March 1, 1831	J. D. Rankin to Margaret Branner
2414	Sept. 27, 1831	Alfred J. Myers to Jane Rheams
2415	June 15, 1831	Mahlon Hammon to Susan Mynat
2416	June 2, 1831	J. M. Carty to Charlotte Reynolds
2417	Feb. 26, 1831	Jeremiah F. Coffew to Melvina Chilton
2418	March 5, 1831	Colonel Branson to Priscilla Varnelle
2419	Jan. 26, 1831	Gillion Lively to Jincey Heaton
2420	Aug. 23, 1832	Isaac Cantrell to Nancy Franklin
2421	April 6, 1832	John Pate to I. C. Wood
2422	May 7, 1832	Wm. Walker to Mary Vance

2423	July 10, 1832	Nathan A. Ballenger to Ruth Bales
2424	June 24, 1832	Benjamine Roberson to Margaret Turner
2425	Sept. 29, 1832	Thomas Davis to Sally Wooten
2426	Aug. 29, 1832	W. C. Jarnagin to Catharine A. Mozier
2427	Aug. 2, 1832	Geo. Weden to Susannah Childers
2428	Sept. 19, 1832	Danil Lyle to Lucinda Mathews
2429	April 14, 1831	Wm. Parks to Mary North
2430	Feb. 7, 1831	Sylvanus Howel to Betsy Ann Cole
2431	Feb. 22, 1831	Hamilton Greenlee to Mary Sunderland
2432	Sept. 20, 1831	Hugh Henry to Elizabeth Jones
2433	Oct. 2, 1831	Wm. Kelsey to Sarah E. Adamson
2434	Nov. 27, 1831	Wm. Brown to Louisa Pitts
2435	Nov. 6, 1831	Jno. M. Patton to Elizabeth Lyle
2436	March 26, 1831	Dard Anderson to Barbara Dobbings
2437	July 2, 1831	Abner Dobins to Manerva Hicks
2438	Feb. 9, 1831	Richard Haworth to Mary Ann Lyle
2439	May 16, 1831	John Bethel to Mary Ballinger
2440	Aug. 31, 1831	Hiram Myers to Mary D. Myers
2441	June 6, 1831	Hezekiah P. Smith to Malinda Lock (no return)
2442	Nov. 23, 1831	John Ursey to Catherine Givens
2443	Nov. 5, 1831	Andrew Witt to Sarah Palmer
2444	Dec. 21, 1831	Silas Cate to Martha Amos
2445	March 21, 1831	Andrew J. Ashmore to Elizabeth R. Snodgrass
2446	Feb. 3, 1831	Daniel McCloud to Elizabeth Garner
2447	March 12, 1831	John G. M. Woods to Susannah Willoughby
2448	Dec. 29, 1831	Jno. P. Bradshaw to Elizabeth Rawlings
2449	Jan. 23, 1832	John G. Boles to Elizabeth Baden (might be Bales)
2450	Nov. 25, 1832	Geo. Burdett to Edith Hockett
2451	Sept. 15, 1832	John U. Dailey to Orlena Cox
2452	Dec. 22, 1832	Thomas Rice to Martha Farmer
2453	Dec. 28, 1832	Valentine Vanhooser to Ame Cooper
2454	Jan. 10, 1832	Thomas Stroud to Nancy Boatman
2455	Dec. 21, 1832	James Coffee to Susannah Coffman
2456	July 21, 1832	Aaron D. Brewster to Catharine Gann
2457	Sept. 24, 1832	Esram Keeney to Polly Moore
2458	July 19, 1832	Preston Reneau to Polly Briant
2459	Dec. 10, 1832	John Vanhooser to Mary Cooper
2460	Nov. 15, 1832	Christopher Williams to Lucinda Nelson
2461	Dec. 14, 1831	Wm. Mills to Mary Hatcher
2462	Nov. 13, 1832	Robert Davis to Tabitha Harris
2463	July 6, 1832	James Quarrillion to Catharine Jones
2464	Dec. 1, 1831	____Chaney to Polly Brazelton
2465	May 9, 1832	Wm. D. Franklin to Sarah Woods

2466	Jan. 8, 1832	John Cate to Rachel Pierce
2467	Nov. 1, 1832	Gillett Malone to Mary Aubrey
2468	Feb. 20, 1832	Japp Mitchell to Sylvanna Presly
2469	Dec. 8, 1832	Dennis Barnes to Rebecca Malone
2470	Sept. 1, 1832	Geo. W. Jones to Elizabeth Bettis
2471	March 27, 1832	Harvey Hodgeon to Mary Neal
2472	Aug. 6, 1832	Madison H. McEffe to Eliza Jane Peck
2473	Feb. 8, 1832	John Pate to Rebecca McCullough
2474	Sept. 13, 1832	Brooks Bennet to Mary Ann Wilson
2475	Aug. 24, 1832	Wm. Walker to Mary Cliff
2476	Jan. 25, 1832	Phillip Mattsbarger to Catharine Newman
2477	Dec. 9, 1830	Abraham Kelly to Mary Ballard
2478	Sept. 17, 1832	Thomas Russell to Mary Elvina Holdaway
2479	June 24, 1832	John Large to Mary Routh
2480	Dec. 21, 1831	John Johnston to Lila Church
2481	April 11, 1831	John H. Farmer to Sarah Douglass
2482	Feb. 11, 1832	Charles Slagle to Leah Lewis Denton
2483	May 28, 1832	Jesse Woodward to Rhoda Morgan
2484	April 19, 1832	Wm. Coward to Mary Smith
2485	Aug. 13, 1832	Thomas Barley to Belona Franklin
2486	Aug. 11, 1833	Wm. D. Moffett to Sally Moree
2487	Sept. 21, 1833	Thomas Dafron to Sea Davis
2488	Nov. 7, 1833	Ben Webb to Hannah Brazelton
2489	Nov. 30, 1833	Wm. Watkins to Flora McKinney
2490	Sept. 25, 1833	Arthur Bond to Sally McAnnelly
2491	March 19, 1833	Joseph Taylor to Sally McCarmick
2492	April 3, 1833	Andrew B. Givens to Margaret Churchman
2493	Oct. 3, 1833	Thomas Burchell to Barbara Hollow
2494	May 16, 1833	Jeremiah Mangrew to Lucrecu Hawn
2495	Oct. 4, 1833	Thomas W. Inman to Edney Austin
2496	Dec. 20, 1833	Wm. Trotts to Elizabeth Martin
2497	Nov. 20, 1833	Jacob Knight to Rebecca Little
2498	Feb. 23, 1833	John Gray to Priscilla Garrett
2499	Aug. 17, 1833	Francis Boyd to Mary B. Ward
2500	Oct. 25, 1833	Wm. M. Kirkpatrick to Naomi White
2501	July 20, 1833	W. H. Steele to Mary M. Blackburn
2502	July 31, 1833	Wm. Haun to Catharine Horner
2503	Aug. 2, 1833	Thomas G. Eckel to Arobel Riggs
2504	Jan. 1, 1833	Wilson Latham to Jane McKinney
2505	Dec. 25, 1835	John Moore to Vina Morris
2506	Oct. 24, 1833	Mecha Staples to Aleander McClannahan
2507	June 13, 1833	Andrew Blackburn Edgar to Margaret Stephens
2508	July 29, 1833	Levi Satterfield to Martha McCarty
2509	July 20, 1833	Daniel G. Park to Mary U. Denton
2510	March 23, 1833	Thomas J. Newman to Maurning Mattox
2511	Sept. 1, 1833	Geo. W. Jones to Eliza Bettis

2512	Dec. 20, 1833	W. L. Henderson to Rebecca Ivy
2513	July 20, 1833	Joseph Wooten to Elizabeth Smelley
2514	Oct. 25, 1833	Frederick Scruggs to Margaret Kimbrough
2515	July 15, 1833	Robert Jones to Caroline Night
2516	Jan. 11, 1833	Wm. Pangle to Catharine Kirkpatrick
2517	Aug. 28, 1833	Thomas Tucker to Elizabeth Hutson
2518	July 27, 1833	Elijah A. Carson to Sarah L. Keith
2519	Oct. 28, 1833	Alfred White to Lociney Welch
2520	June 10, 1833	A. Williams to Hannah Read
2521	April 13, 1833	James W. Inman to Anna J. Lea
2522	Sept. 16, 1833	Joseph C. Bradshaw to Sarah G. Blackburn
2523	March 23, 1833	Wm. Bailey to Margery Coppuck
2524	April 13, 1833	James A. Smith to Permelia Lynch
2525	May 27, 1833	Michael Cate to Mary French
2526	Dec. 10, 1833	Jacob Bell to Patty L. McDaniel
2527	July 20, 1833	Joseph Patton to Wrely Wilhite
2528	Jan. 7, 1833	Austin Hall to Elizabeth Miller
2529	March 16, 1833	Cobb Pierce to Margaret Brown
2530	April 13, 1833	Thomas D. Voss to Lydia Fisher
2531	Oct. 13, 1833	Wm. Brown to Levna Tools
2532	Oct. 15, 1833	Solomon Timmons to Polly Anthony
2533	Jan. 7, 1833	Joseph M. Nolley to Thoda Burnett
2534	Sept. 14, 1833	Allen Harris to Martha Jane Gann
2535	July 1, 1833	Thomas H. McSpadden to Elizabeth Henry
2536	Jan. 13, 1833	Samuel Reed to Rachel Brown
2537	April 15, 1833	Wm. Myers to Martha Collins
2538	Sept. 10, 1833	Jacob G. Thompston to Jane Haworth
2539	Oct. 14, 1830	G. C. Pangle to Elizabeth Langdon
2540	Jan. 9, 1833	Joseph Cate to Sarah Bailey
2541	Jan. 3, 1830	John Cate to Martha Henry
2542	April 2, 1833	Jno. Scribner to Nancy Surratt
2543	March 9, 1833	John Burchfiel to Barbara Brimer
2544	July 25, 1833	David Carter to Polly Carney
2545	Aug. 27, 1833	Wm. M. Barton to Mariah Donaldson
2546	Aug. 17, 1833	Geo. Gregory to Diana Ursary
2547	Jan. 4, 1833	Thomas Gilliland to C. Trevillion
2548	May 18, 1833	John Ellison to Rebecca J. Leath
2549	March 30, 1833	Thomas Ellison to Sally Denton
2550	Sept. 20, 1833	Wm. K. Caldwell to Mariah L. Blackburn
2551	May 23, 1833	William Pack to Ramer Edmonds
2552	Aug. 5, 1833	Benj. Neal to Vicey Ballinger
2553	Sept. 26, 1833	Wm. Morris to Nancy Webb
2554	Jan. 1, 1833	Samuel T. Newman to Mary Ann Elmore
2555	Oct. 16, 1833	John Moyers to Pheobe Ward
2556	Dec. 9, 1833	Thos. Green to Sally Hickey
2557	Oct. 1, 1833	Wm. Williford to Billy Cowan

2558	Sept. 4, 1833	Wm. R. Summon to Betsey Pangle
2559	Jan. 11, 1833	Thos. J. Moore to Caty Eslinger
2560	July 20, 1833	Samuel S. Castillen to Sarah Reeves
2561	Feb. 21, 1833	George Russell to Mary R. Wallace
2562	Sept. 7, 1833	John Martin to Betsey Sparks
2563	Oct. 23, 1833	Archibald Blackburn to Catherine Luckey
2564	Feb. 17, 1833	Isaac Grant to Jane A. Smith
2565	Dec. 28, 1833	Berry Mitchell to Elizabeth Blakely
2566	March 5, 1833	James Estes to Catharine Sitchenlin
2567	Dec. 24, 1833	John Edwards to Elizabeth Taylor
2568	Nov. 22, 1833	John Renfro to Bulah Hawkins
2569	July 16, 1833	W. Baker to Charlotte Morris
2570	Feb. 14, 1833	Jas. W. Greenlee to Edna Sunderland
2571	Dec. 2, 1833	James Maddox to Sarah Johnson
2572	April 21, 1833	Thomas A. Brown to Margaret Blakeley
2573	Nov. 20, 1833	Bradley Kimbrough to F. Cason
2574	Sept. 26, 1833	Christopher Rankin to Francis Galbreath
2575	June 25, 1833	Doctor Crampton S. Harris to M. T. McFarland
2576	Dec. 25, 1833	John A. Salton to Permelia Davis
2577	Dec. 19, 1833	Benj. Inman to Anna Carson
2578	March 20, 1833	Merchent Hawkins to Elizabeth Wilson
2579	June 23, 1835	Henry Scruggs to Margaret Carson
2580	June 21, 1835	Samuel Coffman to Mary Davis
2581	March 23, 1835	Alfred Slover to Cinthia Moore
2582	Aug. 5, 1835	Eli Hammond to Penelope Mitchell
2583	Aug. 10, 1833	James Faun to Jane Jones
2584	Nov. 18, 1835	John Miller to Dorcas A. Rogers
2585	July 10, 1835	Allison Ryans to Amy Briant
2586	Feb. 14, 1835	Wm. M. Mitchell to Penelope Britain
2587	May 6, 1835	John L. White to Desdiona Evans
2588	May 6, 1835	David Barton to Celia J. Donaldson
2589	Aug. 6, 1835	Shadrack Edmonds to Rachel Russell
2590	May 6, 1835	Carr Bailey to Mary Copick
2591	Feb. 11, 1835	Richard W. Vandyke to Lucinda Carter
2592	July 9, 1835	Alfred Martin to Eliza Knight
2593	Sept. 10, 1835	Arthur L. C. Garret to Priscilla Camerson
2594	Dec. 26, 1835	S. C. Morris to M. F. Hazelwood
2595	May 4, 1834	Dulany Gloom to Perlina Gloom
2596	Aug. 1, 1834	Elisha Rogers to Mary Slaton
2597	Feb. 11, 1835	Richard W. Vandyke to Lucinda Carter
2598	Dec. 24, 1834	John Wright to M. Medkiff

2590	Aug. 30, 1834	Martha Hammond to Mary McGhee
2599	Jan. 25, 1834	Jno. H. Gist to J. Love
2600	Feb. 19, 1834	Wm. Atchley to Anna Bowers
2601	Dec. 22, 1834	Haynes Walker to Louisa Moore
2602	Nov. 2, 1834	John M. Patton to Eddy Leons
2603	Sept. 4, 1834	John Hill and Mary Clover
2604	Dec. 3, 1834	Wm. T. Mount to Alizra Cate
2605	Dec. 25, 1834	Augustus French to Keziah Willcocke
2606	July 12, 1838	John Lenox to Mathlda Acoles
2607	Aug. 12, 1834	James A. Coffin to Margaret Martin
2608	Feb. 27, 1834	Jos. A. Malcom to Mary W. Caldwell
2609	Aug. 18, 1834	Wm. Coffman to Mary Ann Churchman
2610	Oct. 4, 1834	William Trevillion to Sophia Gilliland
2611	Jan. 28, 1834	Vincent McKinney to Nancy Newton
2612	Dec. 15, 1834	Raleigh Stubblefield to Unicy Jarnagin
2613	Jan. 7, 1834	Job Parrott to Sallie Smith
2614	Jan. 5, 1834	Alvah McSpadden to Sarah C. Meek
2615	June 5, 1834	Michael Wells to Susannah Cowan
2616	Oct. 16, 1834	Elkanat Hall to M. B. Willoughby
2617	Feb. 24, 1834	Joseph Rutherford to Maude Hays
2618	Jan. 16, 1834	Simeon Griffin to Eliza Dobbins
2619	Feb. 1, 1834	Joseph S. McAndrew to Elizabeth Doherty
2620	June 1, 1834	Joseph Farmer to Susannah Kerwitt
2621	Jan. 29, 1834	James Blakely to Sarah Dick
2622	Jan. 25, 1834	Wm. Reneau to Julian Miller
2623	Nov. 15, 1834	David Gass to Nancy Greenlea
2624	Aug. 18, 1834	Elijah Cross to Arsena Taland
2625	Jan. 27, 1834	Samuel Breaden to Susannah Crobagged
2626	Jan. 31, 1834	Patrick Elliott to Mahla Cowan
2627	Feb. 5, 1834	John Hamlet to Elizabeth Dofron
2628	Nov. 22, 1834	James L. Harvey to Sarah Martin
2629	Dec. 2, 1834	James McBride to Nancy Duncan
2630	May 18, 1834	Robert H. Scott to Prudence Brazelton
2631	May 9, 1834	F. Gregory to Ester Braff
2632	Feb. 15, 1834	Thomas Hazelwood to Mary Randolph
2633	Sept. 8, 1834	George Averet to Ester White
2634	Jan. 31, 1834	Joseph McKinney to Felia Gregory
2635	Dec. 27, 1834	Reuben Tankersley to Emeline Wilson
2636	Feb. 6, 1834	Merrida Williford to Betsey Summers
2637	Oct. 3, 1834	Davis Caldwell to Mary Blackburn
2638	Dec. 9, 1834	Joseph Carmichael to Sarah McDonald
2639	Sept. 15, 1834	John F. Rhoton to Juliet Peck
2640	Oct. 14, 1834	Samuel A. Houston to Letitia Talbot
2641	Oct. 8, 1834	Hiram Todd to Elizabeth Tyler
2642	March 11, 1834	Rufus Keith to Nancy Middleton

JEFFERSON COUNTY MARRIAGES

2643	Oct. 18, 1834	Aramah Hill to Nancy Austell (Austell)
2644	May 13, 1834	W. Fielden to Mary Grams
2645	March 11, 1834	Nathaniel Hood to Isabella W. Edgar
2646	June 6, 1834	John Chilton to Penelope Shelley
2647	Jan. 9, 1834	Jno. F. Holdon to Mary Lane
2648	June 2, 1834	Wm. R. Gwinn to Lucinda Pague
2649	Jan. 20, 1834	Daniel Janeway to M. Lewis
2650	April 7, 1834	Wm. Southerland to Julia Brock
2651	April 1, 1834	Allen Bettis to Catherine Witt
2652	Sept. 22, 1834	Thomas Evans to Loutitia M. Bradford
2653	Dec. 2, 1834	James Allen to Rachel Smelser
2654	Jan. 25, 1834	Edward D. Snoddy to Mary Biddle
2655	May 30, 1834	Louis F. Leeper to Lucinda Jarnagen
2656	Oct. 29, 1834	Jno. O. Green to Mary Middleton
2657	April 17, 1834	Jno. Whalen to Elizabeth North
2658	Oct. 7, 1835	Robert Rollins to Polly Bishop
2659	Jan. 30, 1835	Will Bewley to L. A. Peck
2660	Jan. 29, 1834	Jezekiah Robertson to Delilah Hunt
2661	Aug. 1, 1834	Jonathan S. Ward to Eliza S. Patton
2662	Feb. 7, 1834	Joseph Worley to Jane Brown
2663	March 8, 1834	Isaac Coffman to Phoebe Mekee
2664	May 24, 1834	Chas. Flowers to Sarah Watkins
2665	Nov. 19, 1835	Sterling Hudson to Elizabeth Haynes
2666	Aug. 18, 1858	Thomas T. Kelly to Zilpha Ramsey
2667	Dec. 20, 1855	Wm. Trott to Elizabeth Martin
2668	Sept. 29, 1835	Jacob Carwill to Sarah Copeland
2669	April 6, 1835	Wm. Evans to Elvira Matilda Gwinn
2670	July 6, 1835	Allen B. Mathes to Elvira L. Witt
2671	Sept. 8, 1835	Joseph McKinney to Sophelia Gregory
2072	Nov. 14, 1835	Walden Ballard to Betsy Newman
2673	Aug. 8, 1835	Jeremiah Walker to Martha Davis
2674	May 18, 1835	John Brimer to Mincy Carmichael
2675	Oct. 31, 1835	Abel McCarty to Katy Berry
2676	Oct. 24, 1835	Wm. Dunwoody to Nancy Rankin
2677	Jan. 1, 1835	John R. Chambers to S. Huff
2678	Sept. 12, 1835	Wm. Dawson to Hannah Hale
2679	Feb. 25, 1835	Wm. Pruet to Mary Romine
2680	Sept. 1, 1835	Geo. W. Newman to Mahala A. A. Eaton
2681	Feb. 6, 1835	William Howard to Malinda Gwinn
2682	Sept. 1, 1835	Wm. Tyans to Rebecca Cox
2683	Dec. 17, 1835	Barnabas Riot to Jane Cooter
2684	Oct. 29, 1835	Joseph B. Churchman to Harriet Mynatt
2685	Sept. 7, 1835	Ahaz Johnson to Eliza Stephenson
2686	Oct. 27, 1835	Fleming Pate to Jane Hammons

2687	Oct. 20, 1835	Wm. Kelly to Orena Riggins
2688	Sept. 2, 1835	Jno. B. C. Helm to Ruth Nicholason
2689	Oct. 30, 1835	Wm. T. Hudson, Jr. to Nancy White
2690	Nov. 27, 1835	Richard Hale to Mary Cunningham
2691	July 12, 1835	Jacob Kinser to Nancy Walton
2692	May 14, 1835	Alex Moore to Elender Moore
2693	April 11, 1835	Alex. McCoract to Mina (Mira) Davis
2694	Aug. 26, 1835	Shadrack Manon to Elizabeth French
2695	June 7, 1835	William C. H. Newman to Rachel Bowers
2696	April 4, 1835	Wm. Cluck to Mary Cluck
2697	Aug. 20, 1835	Chas. E. Eckel to Nancy Thomas
2698	April 22, 1834	Hezekiah Chaney to Parthena Poindexter
2699	March 5, 1835	Madison Newman to Mary Ann Kelly
2700	Dec. 29, 1835	Peton Carter to Lucinda Endaley
2701	July 8, 1835	Joseph Wise to Mary Sartain
2702	April 2, 1835	Benj. Wise to Polly Anderson
2703	Oct. 24, 1835	Andrew Coffman to Betsey Tyler
2704	Dec. 17, 1835	Nicholas Long to Jane Coller (Cooler)
2705	Dec. 30, 1835	Alfred McCalanahan to Nancy McClanahan
2706	Dec. 29, 1835	Alex. P. Patterson to Matilda Keeney
2707	Nov. 8, 1835	Jno. A. Little to Elizabeth Johnston
2708	Aug. 24, 1835	M. A. J. Miles to Esther Drinen
2709	Dec. 1, 1835	James Hayes to Dorcas Moore
2710	Nov. 19, 1835	Sylvannus Kanoyler to Hannah Bare
2711	Aug. 4, 1835	Pleasant Cannon to Francis Fuller
2712	May 7, 1835	John Sartain to Milly Williams
2713	Oct. 27, 1835	Daniel Bunch to Nancy Beason
2714	March 2, 1835	John Cowan to Margaret Seahorn
2715	May 4, 1835	Abraham Miller to Elizabeth Miller
2716	Dec. 24, 1835	T. Summitt to Elizabeth Rader
2717	April 16, 1835	Thomas Clevenger to Patsy Neal
2718	Sept. 9, 1835	Lewis Bradshaw to Catherine Lamon
2719	June 13, 1835	James Love to Catherine Lacey
2720	Jan. 13, 1835	Samuel Mitchell to Harriet Cavender
2721	March 15, 1835	Owen Bales to Elizabeth Pite
2722	July 15, 1835	James Love to Jane Henderson
2723	Dec. 21, 1835	Wm. Landrum to Martha Ann Owens
2724	March 28, 1835	Hamilton Gwinn to Charity Coppock
2725	Jan. 22, 1835	James S. Outer to Mary Webb
2726	Nov. 24, 1835	Wm. Wyatt to Rebecca Hill
2727	Aug. 1, 1835	James Talbott to Betsy Wooten
2728	April 15, 1835	Miles F. Scruggs to Jane H. Carson
2729	Aug. 20, 1835	O. K. McClanahan to Alfa Ward
2730	Aug. 21, 1835	B. Ward to A. Harrell
2731	Jan. 22, 1835	Glairbone Lyle to Mary Cannon
2732	March 29, 1835	Abednego Manard to Anegline DeWitt

2733	Nov. 28, 1836	Joseph Johnson to Catherine Newman
2734	Jan. 21, 1836	A. C. Tally to Jane O. Campbell
2735	Jan. 4, 1836	Isaac Childers to Charlotte Turner (Lewis)
2736	Aug. 22, 1836	Allen Crouch to Jane Hickman
2737	Dec. 27, 1836	Joshua Cate to Eliza Tankersley
2738	July 1, 1836	Jonathan Nelson to Rebecca Neal
2739	March 29, 1836	Jacob Davis to Ann Thomas
2740	March 22, 1836	Wilson Shadden to Elizabeth Geuing
2741	Feb. 21, 1836	Geo. W. Routh to Catherine Rankin
2742	March 18, 1836	Murphy Boatman to Elizabeth Cox
2743	Aug. 5, 1836	Andrew Goforth to Laura M. Maynes
2744	Feb. 2, 1836	Andrew Large to Zimly Price
2745	Feb. 8, 1836	Jeremiah Knight to Aloy Gilliland
2746	Aug. 9, 1836	Joseph Anderson to Phoebe Harley
2747	Feb. 14, 1836	Wm. Jones to Elizabeth Reece
2748	Sept. 29, 1834	Allen Hightower to Elizabeth Kimbrough
2749	June 25, 1836	John Jones to Lissa Miller
2750	Feb. 13, 1836	William Rankin to Susan Kimbrough
2751	Aug. 13, 1836	James B. Tanner to Elizabeth Rogers
2752	Sept. 1, 1836	Phillip Travis to Sarah Morris
2753	Nov. 19, 1936	Noah White to Cassandra Kirkpatrick
2754	Feb. 1, 1836	Andrew Jones to Nancy Kimbrough
2755	March 17, 1836	Ellis Walker to P. Coppock
2756	Aug. 21, 1836	James Thomas to Julis Ellison
2757	Jan. 31, 1836	Jonathan Pierce to Rachel Cate
2758	April 7, 1836	David Carr to Elizabeth Ferguson
2759	Jan. 12, 1836	Joseph Cooter to Margaret Staples
2760	Jan. 19, 1836	W. C. Cox to Penelope Pulliam
2761	July 2, 1836	James Curry to Emeliye Chaney
2762	Feb. 17, 1836	Jno. W. McAndrew to Hannah Davis
2763	May 3, 1836	A. B. Anderson to Martha Todd
2764	July 20, 1836	Nathaniel Dunlap to Sallie Henry
2765	July 22, 1836	Thomas Biddle to Sarah Boulder
2766	Feb. 16, 1836	Wm. Harrison to Elizabeth Carson
2767	Nov. 3, 1836	Jno. Newman to Lucinda Coppick
2768	Sept. 5, 1836	Matthew Robinson to Sarah Lindsay
2769	April 17, 1836	Lee Jones to Elizabeth Rickett
2770	Aug. 23, 1836	Aaron Newman to Cassnadra Branner
2771	Feb. 18, 1836	James Koker to Elizabeth Smith
2772	Nov. 12, 1836	Wm. Breedeh to Martha Bile
2773	March 5, 1836	Pleasant T. Jarnagin to Emaline Riggs
2774	June 3, 1836	James Skeen to Sarah Cannon
2775	Oct. 2, 1836	George Rightwell to Rachel McClister
2776	April 3, 1836	Vaichel Hickman to Dalfy Bales
2777	Nov. 9, 1836	Wiley Pullen to Mariam Horner
2778	Sept. 20, 1836	Calvin Patton to Jane L. Thornburgh
2779	Sept. 22, 1836	James Britain to Desdemons Rayl
2780	April 29, 1836	Benj. Cheldrip to Nancy Toale

2781	Oct. 20, 1836	Wilson C. Witt to Roselina Bettis
2782	June 6, 1836	Jesse T. Reed to Sally Reed
2783	April 1, 1836	Benj. Doughty to Rebecca Mathes
2784	April 9, 1836	Beverly Tally to Dorcas McFarland
2785	March 1, 1836	James Henderson to Leah L. Swann
2786	Feb. 27, 1836	David Pierce to Ruthie Campbell
2787	Feb. 2, 1836	Jacob C. Smith to Catharine Jarnagin
2788	Oct. 10, 1836	Sampson Starr to Anna M. Scaggs

INDEX

Ashmore (cont.)
Dorcas 37
Elizabeth 36
Peggy 27
Rechal 42
Sally 33
Atchley, Martin O. 43
Wm. 56
Atkins, Nancy 37
Polly 20
Atkinson, Elizabeth 34
Wm. 27
Aubrey, Mary 53
Austell, Elizabeth 51
Nancy 57
Austen, C. 25
Joseph 30
Austin, Archibald 40
Edney 53
Maria 37
Polly 39
Sarah 1
W. 19
Wm. 34
Auts, Elizabeth 22
Averet, George 56
Axen, James 13
Ayes, David 16
Bacholar, Lucy 44
Backholder, John 10
Baden, Elizabeth 52
Bailey, Carr 55
Celia 43
Charity 4
Elenor 47
Elizabeth 10
James 40
Sarah 54
Wm. 54
Bainwater, Catherine 42
Baker, Agnes 12
Betsy 4
Elijah 18, 49
George 19
John 18, 24, 32
Jos. 40
Mary 3, 16
Nancy 7, 22
Patsy 7
Peggy 22
R. J. 37
Samil 45
Samuel 5, 22
Thomas 29
U. 34

Baker (cont.)
W. 55
Wm. 6, 9,. 44
Balch, James P. 32
Rachel 18
Baldridge, Francis 39
Sarah 46
Baldwin, Margaret 29
Bales, Calvin 48
Dalfy 59
Hampton 20
Henry 38, 46
John 31
John G. (see Boles)
Lidia 32
Mary 46
Nancy 31, 41
Owen 58
Pleasant 43
Polly 35, 41
Rachel 22
Robert 43
Robt. 45
Ruth 52
Susannah 43
Thomas 13
Walter 39
Wm. 23. 34
Baley, Jesse 44
Balinger, John 34
Martha (see Barenger)
Moses 5
Thomas 9
Balkin, Thomas 16
Ballard, Isaah 29
Mary 53
Walden 57
Ballenger, Nathan A. 52
Ballinger, John 8
Lydia 37
Mary 52
Moses 12
Nancy 39
Vicey 54
Bams, Abraham 24
Bane, Adam 26
Baninger, Rachel 43
Bankerston, James 32
Banner, Christiana 43
John 26
Bant, Jenny (Beny) 8
Banton, John 26
Barclay, Martha 5
Bare, Andrew 32
Catherine 39

Bare (cont.)
  Elizabeth 38
  Hannah 58
Barenger, Martha (Balinger) 28
Baringer, Catherine 42
Barker, Agnes 9
  Sarah 8
  Stephen 32
Barley, Thomas 50, 53
Barne, Nancy 21
Barnes, Dennis 53
  Jacob 27
  James 8
  John 21
  Milly 21
  Moses 29
  Peggy 8
  Polly 13
  Sarah 50
  T. 23
Barnet, Michael 28
Barnett, Edward V. 46
  Frederick 15
  Patsey 26
  Polly 31, 31
  Rachel 38
  Sallie 23
  Wm. 48
Baron, Amon 24
Barton, David 55
  Elizabeth 10
  Hannah 28
  Isaac 6
  Jenny (see Sarton)
  Martha 1
  Mary 16
  Sarah 17
  Wm. M. 54
Bates, Anne 22
  James 13
  Martha 46
  Polly 25
Baton, Sarah 48
Battom, Prudence 9
Bayless, Lidia 26
Beaker, Rutha 13
Bear, Jacob 11
  John 30
Beard, Patsy 15
Bearden, Sallie L. 28
  William 22
Bearman, Jane 47
Beason, Nancy 58
Beates, David 27
Beatis, William 25

Beavard, Margaret (Brevard) 19
Beaver, Betsy 14
Beavers, F. 15
Beazley, Hiram 27
Beck, David 11
Becknell, Daniel E. 31
Been, John N. 8
Beline, Mina 16
Bell, Edmond 25
  Elizabeth 36
  Jacob 54
  Jno. 4
  Mary 37
  N. 32
  Sally 4, 28
  Wm. 18
Bennet, Betsey 32
  Brooks, 53
Bennett, McCryer 50
  Rebecca 28
Benton, Jacob (Denton), Jr. 31
  Peter 47
Beny, Jenny (see Bant)
Benyan, Sarah 41
Berger, Polly 34
Berry, Katy 57
  Robert 3
  Thomas 15
Bethel, Austin 49
  Catharine 39
  John 52
  Wm. 35
Bettis, Allen 57
  Bradley 19
  Eli 29
  Eliza 53
  Elizabeth 53
  John 36
  Roselina 60
  Sallie 12
  Samuel 36
  Thomas 35
Bevely, Mary 9
Bewley, Will 57
Beyless, David 2
Bicknell, James 35
Biddle, Margaret 6
  Mary 57
  Thomas 59
Bidwell, Sally 11
Biggs, Alexander 22
  Elizabeth 29, 35
  James 28
Bile, Martha 59
Bimbro, Thomas (Kimbro) 28

Bingham, Lucy 11
  Margaret 5
  Nannie 23
  Samuel 5
Birch, Elijah 39
Bird, Jesse 2
  Nancy 12, 15
Bishop, James 23
  John 37
  Polly 57
  Sally 30
Bittle, Mary 26
Black, Betsy 41
  David 3
  Jacob 20
  Isaac 39
  John 5
  Phebe 40
  Wm. 39, 49
Blackburn, Alex. 41
  Andrew 10
  Archibald 55
  Benjamine A. 42
  Catherine 36
  Cordilla 46
  David 3
  Edward 13
  Elizabeth 13
  Elvira 47
  Frankey 29
  George 8
  Gideon 1
  Grizzy 1
  James 14, 32
  Jennie 15
  Jno. 10
  John 43
  John N. 50
  Malinda 47
  Mariah L. 54
  Mary 50, 56
  Mary M. 53
  Millie 18
  Nancy 13
  Patsey 14
  Peggy 34
  Rebecca 18
  Rosana 44
  Sally 29, 49
  Sarah G. 54
  Wm. 6
Blackstone, Allie 23
  Harvey 23
  James 13, 26
  Patsy 15

Blackwell, Joab 34
  Julius 32
Blagg, Joseph 36
  Sarah 31
Blair, Mary 4
  Unia 28
  Vnus 25
  Wm. 50
Blake, Benj. 22
Blakely, Elizabeth 55
  James 56
  Margaret 55
Blanner, Nancy 12
Blowons, John 31
Blue, John 31
Boatman, Keziah 38
  Murphy 59
  Nancy 45, 52
Boem, Jenny 49
Boiley, Betsy 45
Bolden, William 24
Boles, John G. (Bales) 52
  Julia Ann 44
Bolin, Hannah 39
  James 39
Boling, Washington 44
Bond, Arthur 53
Bone, Adam 30
  Marty 13
Bonman, Simmons 39
Booker, A. 4
Bottom, James 41
  William 15
  Sarah 5
Bottoms, Liddie 5
Boulder, Sarah 59
Bowax, Tabitha 11
Bowen, Rebecca 22
Bowerman, David 29
Bowers, Anna 56
  Rachel 58
Bowlin, Jane 48
Bowls, Susan 47
Bowman, Jacob 7
  John 36
Bows, Sally 6
Boyd, Francis 53
  Jenny 4
  John W. 42
Brabson, John 18
Bradberry, Margaret 22
  Nancy 26
Braden, Betsey 44
Bradford, Berry 6
  Hamilton 10, 10

Bradford (cont.)
  Henry 7
  James 10
  Loutitia M. 57
  Napoleon B. 44
Bradley, Lion 3
  Willis James 30
Bradshaw, Christopher 15
  James 8
  Jno. P. 52
  Joseph C. 54
  Lewis 58
  Linea 15
  Patsy 28
  Richard 19
  Samuel 11
  William 5
Bradson, Berry 49
Braff, Ester 56
Bragg, John 32
  Wm. 24
Brake, Mary 45
Branner, Casper 19
  Cassnadra 59
  Elizabeth 30
  George 34
  Margaret 38, 51
  Micheal 25
  Polly 33
  Sally 31
Brannum, John 18
Branon, Wm. (see Branson)
Branson, Colonel 51
  Polly 26
  Rebecca 17
  Wm. (Branon) 41
Branston, Nancy 26
Brant, Wm. (Bryant) 29
Brazell, Polly 16
Brazelton, Eliza 40
  Hannah 2, 53
  Isaac 4, 42
  Jacob 18
  Jane 29
  Polly 52
  Prudence 56
  Rachel 35
  Samuel 33
  Sants 38
  Sarah 38
  William 12
  Wm. 27
Breaden, Joseph 22
  Samuel 56
Breedeh, Wm. 59

Breeden, Richard 29
Bresmet, Owen 7
Brevard, Margaret (see Beavard)
Brewer, C. 28
  James 37
Brewster, Aaron D. 52
Briant, Amy 55
  Eliza 37
  Polly 52
  Rebecca 36
Brice, Nancy 49
Briggs, John 11
Brimer, Barbara 54
  Elizabeth 23
  John 22, 57
  Nancy 24
  Sabra 49
  Sallie 22
  Tutha 24
  Vinyard 24
Brimmer, Peggy 30
Brindle, George 5
Brister, Nancy (Bruister) 35
Britain, Ann 19
  Betsey 20
  Catharine 16
  James 59
  Penelope 55
  William 1
  Wm. 18
Brittain, Benj. 16
  D. 51
  Elizabeth 6
  John 25
  Joseph 13
  Perine 50
  Polly 23
  Ruth 18
Brittner, Elizabeth 43
Britton, Elizabeth 7
Brock, Julia 57
Brooks, Charles 17
  Jennet 20
  Jennie 12
  Martin 31
  Nancy 12, 39
  Wm. 22
Brothers, Polly 4
Brown, A. 16
  Caliborne 9
  Claiburn 36
  Delilah 4
  Edie 22
  Elizabeth 30
  Francis 20

Brown (cont.)
George 37
Gideon L. 51
Henry 12
Hezekiah 15
James 39
Jane 57
John 2, 17, 33, 36
Judah 30
Margaret 54
Mary Ann 36
Phebe 36
Polly 50
Rachel 47, 54
Thirby 7
Thomas 1, 37
Thomas A. 55
William 22
Wm. 52, 54
Brownlow, Manerva 51
Bruce, Elizabeth 20
John M. 48
Margaret 35
Mary 49
Bruister, Nancy (see Brister)
Bryan, Allen 20
Andrew 1
Elizabeth 38, 44
Patty 11
Bryant, Thomas 23
Wm. (see Brant)
Brymer, John 21
Bryson, Jane 20
John 22
Buant, Sarah O. 47
Buckingham, Elizabeth 2
Buckner, John 18
Mary 38
Bugler, Elizabeth 5
Bullard, Christopher 2
Buller, Polly 6 —
Buly, Geo. 43
Bunch, Daniel 58
Martin 51
Patsy 23
Wm. 23
Bunis, Harriet 45
Bunn, James 6
Bunnells, Wm. 36
Burchell, Thomas 53
Burchfiel, John 54
Joseph 47
Burchfield, Robert 43
Burdett, Geo. 52
Burenine, Diana P. 35

Burgiss, James 30
Burkett, Eliza 49
Burn, Phebe 35
Burnet, John 36
Nathaniel 36
Wm. 36
Burnett, James 47
John C. 32
Manah 37
Martha 43
Thoda 54
Burns, Elizabeth 15
Margaret 35
Mary 36
Patrick 4
Burris, William 10
Burrows, Bryant 45
Butery, Wm. 30
Butry, Sally 37
Caffee, James 4
Cain, Thomas 21
Calahan, Thomas 9
Caldwell, A. 24
Catherine 28
David 50
Davis 56
Elexander 12
Isabel M. 42
James H. 36
Jane K. 29
John 21
Margaret (see Coldwell)
Mary W. 56
Samil 49
Sarah 39
Wm. 46
Wm. K. 54
Caldwill, Anthony 43, 48
Callahan, John 43
Mary 38
Rebecca 40
Cameron, Jane 21
Camerson, Priscilla 55
Campbell, Andrew 21
Archibald 15
Betsy 10
Charles 49
Charlotte 8
Daniel 31
David 3, 43
Deliah 12
Dorcas 39
Eleanor 3, 19
Elender 43
Elizabeth 6, 12, 16

68

Campbell (cont.)
  Geo. 48
  James 1, 5
  Jane B. 21
  Jane O. 59
  Jenny 3
  Jno. 4
  John 25, 35
  Margaret 10
  Martha 4
  Mary 30
  Mary E. 46, 46
  Nancy 18
  Nero 15
  Peggy 28
  Polly 37
  R. F. 51
  Ruthie 60
  Sally 21
  Thomas J. 28
  William 2
  Wm. 34
Camrelle, Mary 14
Canaday, Robert 15
Canady, Benj. 35
Canator, Abraham 24
Canay, Margaret 39
Candike, James 41
Canhooser, Isaac 12
Canhoozer, Wm. 28
Canhorn, Hugh 40
Canley, Leah 14
Canner, Elizabeth 21
Cannile, Lavina 39
Cannon, Abner 7
  Alexander 8
  Isaac R. 43
  Jane 45
  Margaret 18
  Mary 58
  Pleasant 58
  Polly L. 35
  Sarah 59
  Thomas 12, 38
  Zachariah 7
Canon, T. 20
Cantell, Ailey (Cantrell) 22
Cantling, John 14
Cantrell (L. Cantrell) 26
  Adam 19
  Ailey (see Cantell)
  Casinbra 31
  Dickson 29
  Hugh 19
  Isaac 57

Cantrell (cont.)
  Martin (see Caontrell)
  Polly 26
  Thos. 36
Caontrell, Martin (Cantrell) 28
Capman, Jarvis 14
Carback, Thomas 45, 46
Cardwell, John 36
Carey, H. 30
Carig, Eliza 33
Carl, Rebecca 19
Carlock, Unnis 3
Carman, Frankey 43
  James 49
  Jean 6
  Wm. 34
Carmcle, Mary (Carmicheal) 34
Carmen, Nancy 27
Carmichael, Betsy 34
  Elizabeth 5
  James 10
  Joseph 56
  Mary 47
  Mincy 57
  Susannah 16, 36
  Thomas 47
  Wm. 42
Carmicheal, Mary (see Carmcle)
Carney, Polly 54
  Susannah 50
Carny, Joseph 50
Carper, Elizabeth 12
  Margaret 18
  Mary 13
  Sally 25
Carr, Benj. 34
  Betsey 51
  David 59
  Elizabeth 47
  John 48
  Jonathan 14
  Sarah 41
Carrady, John 7
Carridine, Parker 7
Carrol, John 21
Carson, Amery 2
  Andrew 3
  Anna 55
  Cynthia 38
  Elijah A. 54
  Elizabeth 59
  James H. 44
  Jane H. 58
  John 6, 11, 13, 15
  Lavina T. 44

69

Coffman (cont.)
Samuel 55
Susannah 52
Thomas K. 48
Wm. 56
Cofman, Isaac 2
Jacob 6
James 39
John 1, 44
Joseph 23
Mary Ann 20
Parthena 42
Samuel 35, 48
Susannah 30
Thomas 24
Wm. 14
Coiles, Martin B. 40
Coldwell, Margaret (Caldwell) 30
Cole, Betsy Ann 52
Coller, Jane (Cooler) 58
Collins, C. 2
Henry 29
Jane 21
John 14
Martha 54
Mary 49
Rebecca 36
Colplant, John 9
Coltharp, Sophia 48
Colvin, Amanda 32
Combs, Deborah 7
Elizabeth 19
Job. 19
Joseph 17
Nelson T. 36
Sallie 15
Wm. 30, 47
Comes, Abraham (Jones) 18
Comish, Thomas 25
Conner, Catherine 45, 46
Conway, William 9
Wm. 39
Conyers, B. 20
Cook, John 35
Cooler, Jane (see Coller)
Coons, Joseph 7
Coontz, Rebecca 14
Cooper, Ame 52
Jesse 41
John 12, 22
Laide 30
Mary 52
Rachel 1
Sally 5
Winney 30

Cooter, Jane 57
Joseph 59
Copeland, Charlotte 20
Dolly 28
Elizabeth 19
Fanny 27
Francis 22
John 15, 27
Joseph 13
Katherine 4
Mary 1
Nancy 6
Nicholas 4
Parthena 37
Polly 43
Sallie 5, 29
Sally 42
Sarah 57
Solimon 2
Solomon 30
Susannah 18, 21
Wm. 26
Wm. R. 41
Copick, Mary 55
Copland, Charlotte 20
Copper, Isaac 12
Coppick, Elizabeth 48
Lucinda 59
Coppock, Ann 41
Isaah 7
Joseph 11
Mary 33
Peggy 25
Susannah 45
Coppuck, Charity 58
Jacob 20
M. 24
Margery 54
P. 59
Coran, Thoedrick 49
Corbet, Martha 27
Corbett, James 26
Polly R. 26
Cordes, Archibald 17
Cornelins, Aaron 18
Cortley, Keziah 14
Cos, Sally 13
Cother, Philip 27
Cotney, Polly 24
Counts, Henry 33
County, Martha 9
Couter, Maria 36
Covey, Joshua 26
Robt. 33
Ruthey 26

Dameron, Betsy 15
  Elizabeth 13
  John 15
  Kittie 19
Danaldson, Wm. 46
Dangston, James 48
Daniel, Darkie 26
  Ester 28
  James 39
  Nancy 12
  Rachel 9
  Rebecca 15, 24
  Stephen 22
  Thomas 43
  Wm., Jr. 27
Danil, Peggy 27
Danis, Lucy 12
Dannel, Patsy 31
Danvman, Polly 14
Darr, Elizabeth 1
  John 38
  Sarah 51
Daur, Edward 20
Davces, James (see Dawces)
David, Elizabeth 1
  James 6
  Jane (Davis) 51
  Leah M. 4
  Nathan 44
  Nelly 34
  Wm. 6, 23, 24
Davidson, Elizabeth 5
  Isaac 45
  James 8, 39
  Richardson 11
  Samuel C. 51
  Wm. 31
Davis, Aloy 50
  Betsy 7, 22
  Daniel 12
  Elias 1
  Eliza 49
  Elizabeth 9, 15, 18, 44
  Hannah 59
  Jacob 59
  James 9, 49
  James (see Dawces)
  Jane 40
  Jane (see David)
  John 39
  L. 48
  Mahala 50
  Maria 19
  Martha 57
  Mary 55

Davis (cont.)
  Mary A. 34
  Mina (Mira) 58
  Nancy 6, 13, 48
  Nicholas N. 35
  P. 34
  Patsy 22
  Permelia 55
  Polly 7, 15, 25
  Rebecca 2
  Robert 52
  Ruth 48
  Sally 42
  Sarah 17
  Sea 53
  Thomas 9, 51, 52
  William 20
Dawces, James (Davces)(Davis) 20
Dawson, Wm. 57
Day, Betsy 34
  David 3
  Elizabeth 8, 38
  Ester 41
  Hannah 15
  Isaac 38
  John 26
  Levi 14
  Mary 14
  Nathaniel 18
  Nehemnah 16
  Stephen 9
  Thomas 43
  Wm. 36, 47
Deammerl, Sally 11
Dean, John 2
  Robt. 5
  Sarah 13
  Wm. 7
Deans, Elizabeth 12
Deaton, Rebecca 12
Dee, Job 45
Dellis, Elizabeth 20
  John 16
  Polly 28
Deneson, Isabella 7
Deniston, Robert 47
Denneston, Joel W. 47
Denniston, John 2
  Margaret 47
Denny, Polly 11
Denson, Joseph 4
Denton, Catherine 3
  Catherine (see Wenton)
  Elizabeth 35
  Joel G. 24

Denton (cont.)
  Jacob, Jr. (see Benton)
  Jean 4
  Joel 22
  Joel R. 49
  John 7
  Josiah 10
  Joseph 4
  Leah Lewis 53
  Margaret 29, 45, 46
  Martin 42
  Mary U. 53
  Mehala W. 46
  Peggy 31
  Polly 7, 45
  Priscilla 36
  Sally 54
  Thomas 35
  William 3
DenWitt, Scynthia 33
Denwoody, John 28
Dernnis, Betsey 25
Derrick, Henry 19
Deskins, Jesse 42
Deweese, Thomas 32
DeWitt, Anegline 58
  Benjamine 9
Dewoody, Patrick 23
Dick, Betsey 40
  Eleanor 38
  Jane 44
  Margaret 43
  Mary 36
  Sarah 56
  Wm. 31
Dickey, John 42
Dickins, Sally 48
Dinnel, Betsy 34
Dobbin, Peggy 15
Dobbings, Barbara 52
Dobbins, Eliza 56
Dobins, Abner 52
Dobkins, Jesse 37
Dodd, James 31
  Mary 51
  Uriah 37
Dodson, Jas. 12
  John 2
  Millie (see Gobson)
Dofron, Elizabeth 56
Dogget, Jesse 35
  Mary 40
  Thomas 38
Doggett, Anne 47
  Isaac 45

Doggett (cont.)
  Jesse 11
  Louise 46
  Miller 16
  Susannah 12
Doherty, Betsy 3
  Catharine 34
  Casander 51
  Celiah 8
  Dorcas 22
  Elizabeth 56
  Geo. (Genl.) 37
  George 15
  James 2, 23
  James T. 50
  Joseph 36
  Nancy 4
  Polly 10, 13
  Priscilla E. 32
  Rachel 2
  Sally 10
  William 5
  Wm. 4, 30, 30, 31
Doke, Thomas 11
Dolan, John 34
Dolen, John 22
Donaldson, Celia J. 55
  Eliza 46
  Elizabeth 38
  Hannibal 50
  James 37
  Jenny 17
  Mariah 54
  Polly 26
Done, Matilda 48
Donelson, Hannah 9
  Mary 5
Donlds, Mariah L. 48
Dood, Sarah 41
Dorrun, Abraham 22
Doss, John 14
  Peggy 15
Doughty, Benj. 60
Douglas, Jesse 41
  Joanna 42
  John 40
  Polly 41
  Samuel 30
Douglass, Alexander 47
  Andrew 46
  Elizabeth 29
  Hepsey 45
  John 14, 21
  Sallie 25
  Sarah 53

Douglass (cont.)
  Thomas 50
Drake, Geo. W. 41, 50
  James 16
Draper, Peggy 24
Drinen, Esther 58
Driner, Richard 14
Drinnen, John 49
  Mary 24
Driskell, Elizabeth 48
  Sarah 5
Driskill, Jenny 8
Drunen, Thomas 8
Dryden, Thomas 33
Duerkin, Eleanor 36
Duinbee, John 29
Duke, John G. 45
  Washington 39
  Wyery 45
Duncan, Dice 8
  Elizabeth 37
  Joel 35
  John 7, 20
  Joseph 25
  Keziah 6
  Martha 51
  Nancy 56
  Wm. 20
Dunlap, Jane 20
  Nathaniel 59
Dunn, Jesse 16
  Mary 42
Dunwoody, Adam 33
  Wm. 57
Dyer, Ephraim 35
  Lucinda 31
  Robert 9
  Stephen 13
  Thomas 15
Ealinger, Betsy 33
Earls, L. 4
Eastep, Amenca 48
Easter, Floyd 25
  Joseph 28, 28
Easterly, Conrad 9
Eastridge, Sally 3
Eaton, Andrew 16
  Elizabeth 29
  Mahala A. A. 57
  Robert D. 11
Ebbs, John 16
  Nancy 9
Eckel, Chas. E. 58
  Thomas G. 53
Eckle, John C. 31

Eckles, Bradley 39
Eddy, Loyd 6
Edgar, Alexander 26
  Andrew 1
  Andrew B. 27, 46
  Andrew Blackburn 53
  Elizabeth 7
  Emaline 45, 46
  Geo. D. 40
  Isabella W. 57
  Mary W. 3
  Peggy M. 24
  Polly R. 32
Edkins, Wm. 34
Edmonds, Ramer 54
  Shadrack 55
Edmunds, Anny 40
Edwards, Betsy 23
  Delia 5
  Edith 27
  Elizabeth 34
  Hannah 9
  John 2, 55
  Sallie 17
  Wm. 42
Eggar, John R. 38
Elder, Charles 39
  H. 25
  John 17
  Hugh M. 45, 46
  Margaret 12
  Rebecca 43
  Robert 10
  William 12
Eleax, Elizabeth 9
Eller, Jacob 20
  Margaret 43
Elley, Isaac K. 5
Elliot, T. W. 22
Elliott, Elizabeth 14
  Jane 13
  Patrick 56
  Polly 13
  Rebecca 11
  Sallie 17
Ellis, Annie 40
  Elizabeth 18
  Huddy 8
  Jenny 1
  Jesse 13
  John 14, 41
  Joseph 12
  L. 6
  Lucrellia 19
  Nancy 30

Ford (cont.)
  Jenny 24
  Joycey 13
  Margaret 32
  Nancy 5
  Sarah 17
Fore, A. P. 33
Foress, Peggy 4
Forman, John 22
Former, M. 44
Forrest, Anna 4
Forrester, Wm. 46
Fortenburg, F. 32
Fortner, Eleanor 18
Fortress, Sarah 20
Foster, Jerusha 41
  Nancy 50
Fowler, Jeligh 2
  Polly 19
Fox, Delilah 7
Frager, Martha 25
Frame, Elizabeth 5
  John 5
Francis, Edward 43
  Elizabeth 44
Frank, Betsy 30
  James 46
  John 41
Franklin, Belona 53
  Caroline 30
  Elizabeth 33, 45
  James D. 37
  Jane 45
  Mulbury 45
  Nancy 51
  Pelina 50
  Robert D. 50
  Robt. D. 45
  Sallie 35, 50
  Wm. 40
  Wm. D. 52
Franner, Catherine 19
Fraser, Presley W. 41
Frazer, Abner 5
  Abraham 25
  Alice 42
  Eliza 16, 20
  Hannah 27
  Mary 42
Frazier, A. 29
  Hannah 29
  James 37, 38
  Jane 16
  Solomon 34
  Thomas W. 7

Frederick, Celia 34
Free, Philip 6
French, Augustus 56
  Catherine 36
  Elizabeth 58
  Lafford 48
  Mary 54
  Ruthey 46
  Simon 48
  Wm. 31, 50
Freshour, George 18
Frey, Henry 41
Frisbee, Josiah 48
  Sally 43
Frizzell, Jacob 42
Fry, Lucinda 37
Fuller, Francis 58
Funderback, Lancy 15
Galbraith, Isabella 11
  James 27
  John 24
  Nancy 9
Galbreath, Ealsey 13
  Francis 55
Gallahan, Thomas 49
Gallahon, James 23
Galliher, Geo. 2
Gallihime, Nancy 23
Galoway, Hannah 44
Gammon, Nathan 38
Gann, A. 25
  Anne 24
  Catharine 52
  John 17
  Martha Jane 54
  Nancy 9
  Sarah Ann 42
Gannon, Andrew 13
  Caleb 3
  John 17
Gardner, James 29
Garland, Jesse 25
Garner, Elizabeth 52
  Sarah 18
Garret, Arthur L. C. 55
  James 34
  Pleasant 19
  Wm. 1
Garretson, Job 30
Garrett, Gray 36
  Priscilla 53
  Sally 3
Garrison, James 2
  Susannah 4
Garritson, John 16

Gasiton, Jeremich 44
Gass, Andrew 23
  David 26, 56
  James 26
  James H. 47
  Jane 49
Gates, Winny 18
Gaut, Bejamine 48
  Charity 38
  Jo. Mathew 51
  John 35
  Robert 34
Gavins, John 8
Gayley, Anne 2
Gear, Gearland 29
Geer, Elizabeth 38
  Sally 39
Gentry, Charles 38
  Elizabeth 50
  Eveline 50
  John 23
  Martha 33
  Martin 50
  Mary 41
  Robert 12
  Silas 25
George, Edward 6
  Jesse 33
  John 27
  Reuben 6
  Samuel 7
  William 15
Georgey, Catherine 30
German, Geo. 3
Gest, Sarah 2
Geuing, Elizabeth 59
Gibbons, Charles 39
  David 32
  Jenny 30
  Mary 19
  William 19
Gibson, Aaron 15
  Abel 19
  Annie 18
  Charity 16
  Dennis 40
  Leroy 50
  Martin H. 47
  Nancy 46
  Valentine 16, 19
  William 5
Gideons, John 47
Gigar, Mary 31
Giger, Henry 31
  John 1, 6

Gigor, George 13
Gilbreath, Mahlon 37
Gililland, Agnes 11
Gillespie, Nancy M. 50
Gilliland, Aloy 59
  Betsey 49
  David 32
  Sophie 56
  Thomas 54
Gingny, Mary 16
Gist, Jno. H. 56
  Nath. 6
  Wm. 48
Given, Joseph 18
Givens, Andrew B. 53
  Catherine 52
  David 22
  Eleanor 37
  Henry 50
  Peggy 43
  Ruth 15
  Thomas 18, 48
Givins, Wm. 28
Glascow, Thomas 36
Glass, Hiram 38
Glendenan, Ester 2
Gliffer, Polly 44
Gloom, Dulany 55
  Perlina 55
Glossip, Ershula 38
  John 50
Goan, Ezekiel 44
  Shadrack 19
Gobson, Millie (Dodson) 10
Goen, Polly 29
  Wm. 6
Goens, Susan 31
Goforth, A. 34
  Andrew 59
  Charles 37
  Nancy 35
  Sarah 49
Goin, Mary 14
Goins, Benjamine 7
  James 26
Golden, Jacob 42
  William 11
Gollaher, Wm. 29
Good, Phoebe 11
Gooden, Eleanor 1
Gowan, Martha 4
Gordon, Charles 21
Gormen, J. 12
Gorshan, Richard 13
Gossip, Ruthie 38

Gowan, Andrew 8
  James 3, 3
  Nancy 29
Grace, Jane 50
  Nancy 22
  Nelly 30
  Rebecca 35
Graham, Eliza 39
  Eliza Ann 51
  George 30, 51
  Hugh 28
  James 25
  Polly 7
  Priscilla 23
Grame, John 31
Grams, Mary 57
Grant, Betsy 35
  David 40
  Isaac 55
  Jane 17
  John 50
  Wm. 33
Graves, Richard 13
Gray, Jesse 40
  John 53
  Margaret 5
  Sallie 26
Green, John 7, 34
  Jno. O. 57
  Sally 37
  Thomas 9
  Thos. 54
Greene, Jane 31
Greenlea, Nancy 56
Greenlee, Alexander 24
  Hamilton 52
  Jas. W. 55
  John 4
Gregory, F. 56
  Felia 56
  Geo. 54
  Joe 46
  Lucinda 46
  Sarah Ann 49
  Sophelia 57
  Susan 47
Greseum, Ezekiel 8
Gresham, Elijah 24
  Joseph 23
  Richard 21
Gridn, Priscilla 21
Griffin, Dillie 16
  Herman 29
  Margaret 33
  Nelson 34

Griffin (cont.)
  Simeon 56
  Thomas 12
  Wm. 47
Grisham, John 8
  John (see Gusham)
  Joseph 35
  Lavina 37
  Michael 27
  Polly 26
  Richard 15
Gussam, Elizabeth 31
Guthre, Anne 29
Grove, Margaret 36
Guinn, Elizabeth 31
  Kesiah 31
Gure, Jacob 30
Gurry, John 14
Gusham, John (Grisham) 26
Gussam, Elizabeth 31
Guthre, Anne 29
Guthrie, James 6
Gwin, John 5
Gwinn, David 47
  Elvira Matilda 57
  Hamilton 58
  John 20
  Malinda 57
  Mary 28
  Wm. 50
  Wm. R. 57
Haburg, Patsy 21
Hacket, Susan 28
Hackley, Juda 2
Hackworth, B. 33
Haddy, Maraga 5
Hadley, Elizabeth 51
Hagans, Alfred 41
Haggard, Florence 11
  Henry 5
  Noah 17
Haill, Samuel 5
Hailey, Polly 23
Hains, Jerry 12
  Wm. 14
Hale, Hannah 57
  Jennie 12
  Patrick 31
  Richard 50, 58
  Thomas 25
Hall, Austin 54
  Elkanat 56
  Jonathan 20
  M. 17
  Marjah 43

Hall (cont.)
  Nancy 9
  S. 26
  Silas 16
  William 17
Hamble, James 33
  Jane 36
Hambrick, Green 15
Hambright, Polly 6
Hamilton, Elizabeth 31
  Jas., Jr. 35
  Mary 38
  Robert 40
Hamlet, Elizabeth 43
  Jane 44
  Nancy 34
  Sarah 49
  Susannah 31
  Wm. 30
  John 56
Hammel, Elizabeth 24
Hammer, Jesse 18
  Jonathan 26
  Lydia 28
Hammil, Alexr 19
Hammock, Pleasant 42
Hammon, Catharine 44
  Elizabeth 14
  Mahlon 51
Hammond, Betsey 43
  Eli 55
  Elizabeth 8
  Martha 56
  Mary 12
  Moses 18
  Rebecca 19
  Thomas 11
Hammonds, Samuel 50
  Wm. 29
Hammons, Jane 57
Hampston, Edward 6
Hampton, Ann 5
Hamson, Hannah 8
Hance, Elizabeth 51
Handerson, Elizabeth B. 27
Handy, John 27
  Rhoda 26
Hanes, Anna 34
  Christopher 17
  Elizabeth (see Henes)
  Michael 24
  Polly 14
  Priscilla 17
  Sally 30
  Thomas 21

Haney, Rebecca 38
Hanker, John 21
Hankins, Deborah 21, 40
  Eli 18
  Rebecca 25
  Susannah 38
  Thos. 17
  Wm. 35
Hanks, Mary 5
Hanly, J. W. 25
Hann, Chaney 45
  Pheba 24
Hanner, Henry 34
Hanney, Nancy 3
Hannonds, Patsy 47
Hanson, Betty 6
  Wm. 44
Harden, James, Jr. 1
Hardy, Susannah 27
Hargrave, Abialla 6
  Eli 2
Harle, Baldwin 35
  Hannah 9
  Harriet 47
  Malinda 45
  Maria 36
  Sally 29
Harley, Phoebe 59
Harman, Elizabeth 44
  Susannah (see Horman)
Harmon, Julianna 32
Harnson, John 49
Harold, Catherine 19
Harp, Asspitis 11
Harrell, A. 58
  Elisha 20
Harris, Allen 54
  Crampton S. (Doctor) 55
  George 20, 32
  Isaac 24
  James 15
  Jane 17
  Jas. A. 48
  Keziah 47
  L. 32
  Lucinda 32
  Martha 43
  Nancy 7
  Phebe 37
  Tabitha 52
  Thankful 3
  Wm. 37
Harrison, Ann 11
  Benj. 20
  Charles 29

Harrison (cont.)
  Delila
  Elizabeth
  James 5, 17
  Jenny 17
  John 16, 18
  Mary 6
  Peter 27
  Polly 18
  Rachel 21
  Wm. 9, 59
Harriston, Sally 33
Harrold, Selah 19
Hart, John 36
Hartgraves, John 26
Harvey, James L. 56
  Robt. 36
  Sally 20
Harvy, John C. 31
Hash, John 23
Hask, Selvy 1
Hasket, John 36
Hatcher, Mary 52
Hathcocke, Thomas 27
Haun, Adam 39
  Alex 48
  Elizabeth 29
  John 50
  Wm. 53
Havard, Charity 13
Hawkins, Bulah 55
  Deborah 8
  Merchant 55
  Thomas 12
Hawn, Lucrecu 53
Haworth, Anne 35
  David 43
  Hannah 23
  Jane 54
  Richard 52
  Sarah 11
  West 36
Hayes, Elizabeth 8
  James 58
Haynes, Elizabeth 57
  John V. 51
  Margaret 49
  Richard 29
Hays, Alexander 14
  Cyms 49
  Easter 4
  Elizabeth 27
  Enoch 39
  John 1, 14, 24
  Maude 56

Hays (cont.)
  Nicholas 38
  Rachel 14
  Suzannah 3
  Sylvy 31
Hazelwood, M. F. 55
  Thomas 56
Hazlewood, Mary Ann 47
Headly, Polly 44
Hearn, Danile 49
Heath, Jowell 50
  Martha 49
Heathcocke, Allen 48
Heaton, Jincey 51
Hebbert, J. 6
Hedrick, Jas. 31
Hegdon, Betsy 36
Helm, Jno. B. C. 58
Helton, Alex 45
  Catherine 29
  Elizabeth 34
  Hannah 38
  James 14
  Vina 15
  Wm. 40
Hembrick, Celia 15
  Wm. 13
Henderson, Andrew L. 28
  Betha 13
  Elizabeth 20, 22
  Flora 32
  Geo. 44
  George 3
  James 60
  Jane 22, 33, 58
  Jenny 1
  John 17, 23
  Joseph 2
  Malinda 21
  Mary 17, 34, 49
  Maston 37
  Nancy 9
  Nolen 33
  Polly 10, 16
  Rachel 39
  Robert N. 39
  Ruth 16
  Sally K. 31
  Thomas 18
  W. L. 54
  Wm. 34
Henes, Elizabeth (Hanes) 17
Henry, Benj. 24
  Elizabeth 54
  Hugh 52

Henry (cont.)
Jno. 3
Martha 54
Mary 20
Sallie 59
Sarah 44
Silas 25, 46
William 21
Henshaw, Lucinda 42
Henshay, Wm. 48
Hensley, Anne 29
Eliza 36
Henson, Martin 43
Herbert, David 2
Herman, Elizabeth 17
Herndon, George 29
Herron, Joseph 47
Hert, Gallant 29
Hervey, Thomas 37
Hester, Ferrell 12
Hewn, Polly 25
Hickey, John 35
Rachel 19
Sally 54
Vetsey 47
Wm. 16
Hickman, Benj. 30
Caleb 17
Darah 47
Francis 6
J. 46
James 5, 45
Jane 59
John 36
Jno. 5
Polly 18, 28
Rebecca 17
Sally 18
Thomas 18, 25
Vaichel 59
Wm. 11, 27, 36
Hicks, Manerva 52
Richard 16
Hide, Leah 17
Higdon, Thomas 37
Hightower, Allen 59
Hill, Abagail 43
Abraham 30
Alex 31
Allen 3
Aramah 57
Elijah 42
Elizabeth 2, 39, 42
Ellender 28
Hannah 28

Hill (cont.)
James 21, 41
Jane 49
Jenny 10
Jesse 13
Jethro 44
John 15, 17, 21, 25, 56
John M. 19
Jonathan 1, 9
Joseph 16
Lavina 51
Polly 5, 12
Rebecca 17, 58
Robert 15
Sally 14, 23
Samuel 3, 21, 21
Sarah 9
Thomas 1
Wm. 34
Hillett, Abner 40
Hillion, Nathan 41
Hinchey, Mary 22
Hobert, Elizabeth 17
Hockett, Edith 52
Hodgan, Mary Ann 19
Hodge, Calloway 44
Charles, Jr. 29
Patsey 41
Rebecca 36
Stephen W. 46, 46
Hodgen, Robert 25
Sallie 14
Sterling 49
Hodgeon, Harvey 53
Hodges, Betsey 12
Callowan 20
Editha 38
Edmund 10
Eliza 41
Francis 50
James 4, 11, 16
Jane 36
John 26
Joseph D. 50
Moses 27
Nancy 6
Pheba 11
Polly (see Rodgers)
Rebeca 24
Rhoda 13
Wm. 8, 12
Ziphin 24
Hoggatt, Sarah 41
Hogin, Darling 37
Hoin, David 2

Hoins, Lyde 24
Holdaway, Mary 45, 46
  Mary Elvina 53
  Nancy 42
Holden, Jno. F. 57
Holdway, Anna 14
  Mary 44
Holeway, Wm. 24
Holland, James 19
Hollow, Barbara 53
Holloway, Any 23
  Fanny 26
  Patsy 22
  Rachel 21
  Sally 33
Holmes, D. 6
  Elizabeth 5
Holston, Henry 49
Homer, Cavalier (Horner) 38
Honore, Susan 9
Hood, Nathaniel 57
  Polly 15
  Robert 23
Hooker, Joseph 42
Hope, Elizabeth 11
Horan, Betsey 25
Horman, Susannah (Harman) 23
Horn, Daniel 29
  James (see Hown)
Hornback, Eli 15
  Jane 15
  Jas. 13
  John 4, 25
  John R. 27
Horner, Betsy 35
  C. H. 29
  Catherine 9, 53
  Cavalier (see Homer)
  Elizabeth 32
  Esther 10
  Fanny 38
  Isaac 27
  John B. 33
  Mariam 59
  Polly 11
  Spencer 33
  Thomas 29
Horton, B. 31
  Thomas 9
Hoskin, William N. 26
Hoskins, Fanny 35
  George 12
  H. 25
  James 11, 50
  Molly 3

Hoskins (cont.)
  Nancy 3
  Patsy 27
  Polly 11
  Sarah 8
  Thomas A. 47
House, Sa-uel 16
Housley, Robert 41
  Thomas 41
Houston, Samuel A. 56
  Mary 8
  William 18
Howard, Alex 6
  Alexander 8
  Blackstone 3
  Elizabeth 28
  Fanny 25
  Jane 23
  Jonathan 26
  Mary 8, 25
  Nancy 25
  Pheba 13
  Polly 3
  Robert 14
  Samuel 26, 29
  Sarah 18
  William 22, 57
Howel, James 13
  Patton 41
  Sylvanus 52
Howell, Asa 35
  Delilah 21
  Jas. O. 44
  Jemima 36
  Malachi 1
  Patsy 36
  Sarah O. 42
  Temperance 37
  Walter 37
Hown, James (Horn) 38
Hudson, James 51
  Sterling 53
  Wm. T., Jr. 58
Hueely, Robert 25
Huff, Keziah 4
  Philip 3
  S. 57
Huffman, John 16
Huggins, Sally 18
Hughs, Jno. 3
Hull, Margaret 19
Humpston, Reuben L. 37
  Susan 31
Hunt, Delilah 57
Hunter, James 4

Johnson (cont.)
Martha F. 38
Mary 2, 39, 50
Mathas 38
Mathews 41
Nancy 22
Polly 27
Preston J. 44
Robert 6
Sarah 55
Stephen 38
Thomas 20
Thomas D. 49
Uniah 16
Wm. 4
Johnston, Elizabeth 58
Jacob 38
James 27
John 53
Margaret 5
Jolly, Abner 43
Joseph 42
Polly 34
Jones, Abagail 40
Abraham (see Comes)
Andrew 59
Anny 7
Betsey 51
Betsy 6
Catharine 52
Caty 50
David 6, 8
Eli 48
Elizabeth 52
Fanny 29
Geo. W. 53, 53
Hannah 6
J. 21
Jane 18, 55
Jeremiah 27
John 59
John G. 40
Joshua 43
Lee 59
Martin 13
Mary 37, 44
Miles 32
Patsey 9, 21
Reps 43
Robert 38, 54
Sally 21
Samuel 13
Sarah 19, 37
Simon 38
Susannah 9

Jones (cont.)
Tamps 17
Thomas 6
William 8, 22
Winney 48
Wm. 13, 59
Juban, William (Julian) 10
Julian, William (see Juban)
Julias, Elizabeth 8
Kamebrer, Kalley 28
Kanayler, Sylvannus 58
Kate, Lucy (Cate) 29
Kedner, Rebecca 42
Keeger, Katherine 4
Keener, John H. 42
Keeney, Abram 44
Esram 52
Margaret 40
Matilda 58
Nancy 29
Sarah 41
Thomas 33
Keeth, Gabriel 11
Keith, Catherine W. 10
Rufus 56
Sarah L. 54
Tabitha 17
Kelley, William 26
Kelly, Abraham 53
Charlotte 48
Elizabeth 24
Enoch 38
Jane 40
Lucretia 19
Mary Ann 58
Robert 18, 43
Sally 7
Thomas 35
Thomas T. 57
Wm. 27, 33, 48, 58
Kelsey, Aaron 37
Elizabeth 39
Hannah 39
Wm. 52
Kelso, Chas. B. 12
Jenny 3
Kenedy, Walter 3
Keney, Jonathan 11
Kennedy, Adam M. 33
Lucas 31
Robert (Kenney) 3
Kenney, Robert (see Kennedy)
Kerr, Andrew 2
Susannah 35
Kerwitt, Susannah 56

86

Ketching, Benjamine 11
Keth, Agnes 5
Ketner, Jonathan 42
  Mary 40
Key, Hugh 20
Keyler, Katherine 7
Kidwell, D. 36
  David 32
  Nancy 47
Killen, Goodwin 17
Kilpatrick, Hugh 1
  Ruth 28
Kimbro, Duke 3
  Isaac 17
  John 8, 26
  Nanny 26
  Thomas (see Bimbro)
  William 19
Kimbrough, B. 15
  Benony 43
  Bradley 44, 55
  David 17
  Easler 43
  Elizabeth 59
  John 17
  Lacy 51
  Margaret 54
  Mary 48
  Nancy 59
  Rebecca 41
  Sarah 45
  Susan 59
  Susan D. 51
  Thomas 51
King, Barnaby 48
  Betsy Ann 41
  Fanny 1
  James 13, 17
  Janet 4
  John 36
  Joseph 36
  Levica 14
  Levice 30
  M. 2
  Martha 41
  Mary 47
  Nancy 37
  Patsy 44
  Robert 49
  Sally 21
  William 15
  Wm. S. 43
Kinkade, John 8
Kinkaid, Jennet 1
Kinser, Jacob 58

Kirk, John 4
Kirkpatrick, Cassandra 59
  Catharine 54
  Elizabeth 33
  Hannah 6
  James 5
  Jane 36
  Jennet 24
  Wilke 9
  Wm. M. 53
Kitccuel, Peggy 6
Kitchen, Ephrain 46
  Susannah 48
Kitrell, Joseph 37
Knave, Mary 20
Knight, Eliza 55
  Jacob 53
  Jeremiah 59
Koker, James 59
Kum, Betsy 3
Labeapeco, Judith 13
Lacey, Catherine 58
Lacy, Elizabeth (see Lracy)
Lackey, Joseph 32, 32
Lain, Easter 25
Lake, Jacob 9
Lamar, Wm. 36
Lambert, Elizabeth 6
Laminore, Geo. 23
Lamon, Catherine 58
Lanan, Sarah M. 35
Landrum, Mary 28, 35
  Wm. 58
Lane, A. 23
  Easther 28
  Eda 42
  Edeline 39
  Elizabeth 22, 26, 42
  Garritt 9
  James 38
  Lear 26
  Mary 57
  Nancy 5, 24
  Nancy Jane 46
  Noah 28
  Penna 25
  Polly 35, 40
  Right 49
  Tidence 29
Langacre, Andrew 12
Langdon, Elizabeth 54
  Jane 27
  Jonathan 30
  Joseph 1
Langford, Sally 30, 32

Lanksle, Matilda 48
Lanmoore, R. 22
Lanson, John 31
Lanston, Polly 20
Lanstone, Hannah 17
Larew, George 10
Large, Adam 49
  Andrew 59
  Jacob 34
  John 53
  Joseph 32
  Lucy 38
  Phebe 35
  Robert 31
  Stephen 51
Larkins, Vincent 5
Larrance, Cynthia 49
  David 39
  John 28
  Polly 43
Larrence, John 35
Larson, Lenny 12
Larver, Lewis 10
Lasent, Lucy 44
Latham, Betsy 37
  Wilson 53
Lathers, Betsy 18
Laurance, Sarah 23
Laverly, Margaret 35
Lawrence, Henry 32
  Jonathan 41
  Mary 33
  Nancy 37
  Rebecca 41
  Sarah 30
Lay, Dorcas 18
  Polly 24
Layman, Anne 21
  David 9
  John 9
  Mary 21
  Nancy 28
  Polly 15
Lea, A. 25
  Anne J. 54
  Elender 3
  Jesse 6
  John 14
  John H. 35
  Major 1
  Mary (see Lee)
  Nancy 14
  Susannah 3
  Wm. 26
Leanna, Kiles (Lyles) 40

Leath, Edith 25
  Jeremiah M. 48
  Josiah 2
  Rebecca J. 54
Leay, John 19
Lee, F. 21
  Leander 48
  Major 9
  Mary (Lea) 35
  Susannah 15
Leeper, Louis F. 57
Leeth, Barbara 7
  Ebenezer 43
  George 30
  Levena 37
Legg, Nancy 22
  Samuel 35
  Wm. 18
Leggett, Wm. 4
Leith, Evenezer 16
  George 7
  Jeriah 49
Lemmons, Barbara 24
Lennon, Rachel 10
Lennox, John 24
  Polly 20
  Sallie 12
Lenox, Anne 29
  John 56
Leons, Eddy 56
Lester, James 2
Leth, Elizabeth 1
Letner, Adam 35
  John 29
Letter, Rebecca 41
Lewes, Betsy 31
  Habriel 21
  James 11
  Nelly 22
Lewis, Charlotte (see Turner)
  David 5
  Dolly 29
  Eli 21
  Enoch 21
  Geo. 49
  George 27
  Henry 32
  Levi 17
  M. 57
  Nancy 42
  Richard 14
  Samuel 42
  Susannah 32
Libarger, Fanny 2
Lichliter, David 31

Lichliter (cont.)
  Deborah 31
  Esther 32
Liggate, Rogert 3
Lile, Abner 32
  Casandra 37
  Ransom 39
Liles, Dolly 34
  Isabella 36
  Mahala D. 32
  Nancy D. 35
Lindsay, Sarah 59
Lindsy, Wm. 39
Line, Elizabeth 26
  John 43
  Mary 19
  Wiley 47
Lingerfeltor, Polly 30
Linsey, Elizabeth 23
Little, Jno. A. 58
  Rebecca 53
  Thomas 8
Lively, Catherine 16
  Dela 49
  Gillion 51
  Joseph 16
  Laretia 39
Lock, Isaac 40
  John 50
  Malinda 52
  Susannah 39
Locke, Em. 46
  Nancy 37
Locket, Sally 29
Lockhart, Elizabeth 46
  John 33, 35
  Polly 25
Long, Arthur 48
  George 17
  Joseph 27
  Margaret 25
  Nancy 35
  Nicholas 23, 34, 58
  Polly 36
Longacre, Ann 12
  Benj. 19
  Betsey 12
  Elizabeth 24
  Hannah 10
  John 31
  Rachel 9
  Richard 24
  Ruth 16
Looney, Peter 2
Loury, Elizabeth 26

Love, Anne 49
  J. 56
  James 58, 58
  John 9
  Lucy M. 25
  Mary Ann 51
  Thomas 39
  William 5
  Wm. 6
Lovey, Ann W. 9
Lowe, Abner 6
  Abraham 44
Lowell, George 21
Lowery, Adam 15
  Betsey 10
  David 10
  Isaac 25
  Peggy 14
  Polly A. 29
  Rebecca 11
  Robert 4, 4
  Samuel 13
  Sarah 13
Lowry, Polly 30
Loyd, Hirma 39
Lracy, Elizabeth (Lacy) 14
Luck, Wm. 17
Lucker, Edith 25
Luckey, Catherine 55
Luttrell, Richard 28
  Wm. 35
Lyle, Daniel 20
  Danil 52
  Elizabeth 51, 52
  Glairbone 58
  Jane 21
  Mary Ann 52
  Samuel 5
Lyles, Elizabeth 48
  Gulda 48
  Leanna (see Kiles)
  Robert 28
Lyman, Chnsie 23
  Jacob 23
Lynch, Permelia 54
Lynn, Lewis 16
Lyon, James 3
Mabee, Lemmel 15
Mackguire, Patience 13
Mackroberts, Mary 7
Macy, John 42
  Jonathan 17
  Rachel 42
Maddox, James 55
Madson, Susan 37

Magers, Dicey 23
  John 6
Magnet, Priscilla 32
Maiden, Betsy 31
  Isaac 31
Maize, Millie 2
Majors, Abner 6
  Elias 10
  Nancy 15
  Peter 5
  Phebe 35
  Polly 7
  William 17
Malcom, Elizabeth 39
  John 8
  Jos. A. 56
  Lidia 26
  Mary 21
  Robert 18
  Wm. 8
Malcourt, Anne 43
Malone, Gillett 53
  Rebecca 53
Maloney, Elizabeth 8
Manard, Abednego 58
  Daniel 45
  Levi 36
  Shadrick 43
  Susannah 16
Mandenhall, Charity 2
Manes, Anes 29
  Richard 22
Mangrew, Jeremiah 53
Mankins, Annie 17
Manley, Daniel 39
  Elizabeth 14, 51
  Polly 41
  Susannah 31
Manly, Elizabeth 46
Mann, Elijah 32
Mannel, C. 4
Manner, Rebecca 40
Manning, N. 28
Manon, Shadrack 58
Mansfield, Anna 30
  Betsey 17
  John 32
  Malinda 42
  Nancy 37
  Polly 30
  Thomas 27
Manson, Betsey 32
Mapes, Rachel 26
Maples, Jennie 29
  Jenny 29

Maples (cont.)
  Jesse 48
  Margaret 8
  Martha 48
  Morgan 40
  Phebe 43
Margreves, Andrew J. 48
Marine, James 50
Markison, John 7
Markland, James 3
  Mary 33
Markman, Ruth 5
Marr, Rdoda (see Mazr)
Marshall, Alex. 30
Martain, Samuel 24
Martin, Alfred 55
  Elizabeth 38, 53, 57
  Elizabeth A. 35
  Hugh 15
  Jane 40
  Jean 43
  John 55
  Lewis, Sr. 47
  Margaret 56
  Mary 34
  Nancy 35, 42
  Robert 39
  Sarah 56
  Tabitha 22
  Thos. J. 31
Mashill, Wm. 24
Mason, Sally 34
Massengill, Elizabeth 45
  Henry E. 51
Massey, Joshua 18
  Susannah 8
Maston, Mariah 44
Mathes, Allen B. 57
  Dorcas 4
  Lavinia 34
  Polly 15
  Rebecca 60
  Thomas 4
  William 18
Mathews, John P. 50
  Lucinda 52
  Samuel 23
  Sarah 16
Mattsbarger, Phillip 53
Mattox, Maurning 53
Mauldby, Wm. 13
Maulsly, Sarah 7
Maxwell, Elizabeth 7
  Isaac 27
  John 23

May, Nelson (see Ivey)
  Priscilla 32
Maye, Caleb 21
Mayes, Joshua (Moyers) 21
Mayfield, Isarel 4
Maynes, Laura M. 59
Mays, Fanny 31
  John 17
  Patsey 29
  Sallie 9
  William 50
Maze, Elizabeth 45
  Lemuel 25
  Priscilla 28
  Wm. 42
Mazr, Rhoda (Marr) 10
McAdro, Samuel 44
Mchafy, Jennie 5
McAndrew, A. 27
  Jno. W. 59
  Joseph S. 56
  Richard 49
  Wm. 45
McAnnelly, Sally 53
McBee, Adam H. 48
McBride, James 56
McBroom, William 15
McBrown, Mary 42
McCall, Hugh 39
McCampbell, John 28
  Wm. 39
McCann, Wm. 14
McCarmick, Sally 53
McCarrol, James 8
McCarter, Abraham 24
  William 22
McCarty, Abel 57
  Martha 53
McCenky, Robertson 39
McClanaham, Alfred 58
  Elizabeth 7, 19, 39
  James 26
  John 24
  Nancy 58
  O. K. 58
  Polly 26
McClanghlind, Polly 11
McClannaban, Mary 46
McClannahan, Aleander 53
  Alexander 13, 23
  David 20
  Elizabeth 23
  Fanny 9
  Isaac 20
  Isabella 51

McClannahan (cont.)
  John 14
  Joseph 16
  Leannah 44
  Nancy 48
  Rebecca 4
  Robert 14
  Wm. 13
McCleany, Polly 43
McClenahan, Levina 37
McClister, James 27
  Jean 26
  John 41
  Polly 25
  Rachel 59
  Sally 27
  Wm. 41
McCloud, Daniel 52
  Patsy 49
McClure, Wallace 4-
  Cyrus 34
McCogg, Thomas 2
McComick, Andrew 45
McConnell, Marjah 38
McCoract, Alex. 58
McCormack, Samuel 3
McCormick, Benjamine 44
McCory, Wm. 32
McCown, Nancy 35
McCoy, James 2
McCrarey, Benj. 33
McCrary, Sally 37
McCray, Henry 49
McCuistain, James 15
McCuistian, James 30
  Jane 39
  Levina 37
  Mary Ann 42
  Robert 14
McCuistion, Andrew 5
  Samuel 3
McCullah, Elizabeth 20, 21
  Jane 44
McCullock, Amy 35
  Jeannette 7
  Wm. 20
McCullough, Rebecca 53
McCurne, Susanah 45
McCustin, Catherine 27
  Joseph 24
McDaniel, Lewis 42
  Mary 47
  Melinda 50
  Patty L. 54
  Wm. 43

McDaniels, Allen 44
McDanil, Jas. 45
McDannel, Mary 50
McDolaid, James 22
McDonald, Alex. 6, 25
  Elizabeth 40
  James 9
  Jene 40
  John 42
  Joseph 11
  Lydia 39
  M. 29
  Margaret 33
  Mary 2, 30
  Paul 5
  Peggy 32
  Polly 11
  Prudence 33
  Robert 41
  Rosanna 3, 30
  Sarah 56
  Susan 29
McDowel, Wm. 30
McDowell, B. 18
  Elizabeth 18
  Minney 34
  Susannah 28
McEffe, Madison H. 53
McFarland, A. B. 24
  Adline M. 49
  Benj. F. 45
  Betsy 15
  Catherine 29
  Dorcas 60
  Isabella 39
  James 5
  John 7
  Lucy 15
  M. T. 55
  Mary 34
  Polly 6, 22
  Rachael 7
  Rachel 33
  Reuben 4
  Robert 14, 28, 33
  Robt. 32
McFarlin, George 1
McGair, Ruth (McGuire) 26
McGangal, Floyd 22
McGee, Sally 4
McGhee, Alex. 35
  Asa 15
  Elinor 12
  James 37
  John 2

McGhee (cont.)
  Mary 56
  Melvina 24
  Millie 11
  Rachel 17
  Sally 33, 33
McGihan, Geo. 3
McGirk, Sally 25
McGirt, Elizabeth 10
  Margaret 13
  Polly 25
McGlocklin, Alex 21
McGlosthlin, Susy 3
McGlowan, Nancy 42
McGowan, Nancy 33
  Sarah 35
McGoys, Margaret 43
McGrennigel, Margare 16
McGuffin, Hugh 24
  Jane 21
McGuin, Randolph 34
McGuire, Annie 13
  Catherine 10, 35
  Charles 10
  Elizabeth 32
  Joseph 21
  Lydia 50
  Mary M. 20
  Michael 33
  Nancy 9, 22, 25
  Rachel 24
  Ruth (see McGair)
  Thomas 42
McKaney, Alexander 13
McKee, Elizabeth 51
  Levicy 47
  Nancy 36
  Wm. 48
McKinney, Barbara 37
  Dandridge 31
  Fanny 47
  Flora 53
  Jane 53
  Lampkin 34
  Joseph 56, 57
  Martha 46
  Nancy 35
  Rachel 47
  Sarah 37
  Vincent 56
  Wm. 25, 35
McKinny, C. 21
McKnight, Elinor 33
  Mary 32
  Thomas 29

McLanakan, Frances 36
McLow, John 6
McLung, James 21
McMahon, Wm. 1
McMarland, Jas. 48
McMean, Isaac 14
  Peggy 22
  Rebecca 13
McMeans, Susannah 6
McMeen, Susannah 16
McNeal, Sarah 21
McNeely, Nancy 15
McNice, Wm. 41
McNiel, John 25
McNight, Grace 18
  John 23
McNiston, Margaret 40
McPherson, Samuel 10
McQucan, Rebecca 8
McQuster, James 31
McRoberts, Samuel 2
McSpadden, Alvah 56
  Dorcus 23
  Easter B. 23
  Elizabeth 20
  Ester 46
  James 13
  Jennie 15
  John 19
  K. 27
  M. H. 44
  Martha K. 48
  Mary 19
  Nancy 9
  Peggy 28
  Polly V. 43
  Sally 25
  Samuel 7, 29, 33
  Thomas A. 48
  Thomas H. 54
  Thos. 17
Meadows, Hilly 27
  Jane 50
  Polly 38
Meals, Daniel 20
  Jennet 14
  Naney 26
  Sally 23
  Wm. 30
Medkiff, M. 55
  Polly 33
Medlow, Nancy 44
Meek, Adam K. 33
  Charles 6
  Jane 31

Meek (cont.)
  Sarah 15
  Sarah C. 56
Meels, John 11
Meger, Abraham 13
Mekse, Phoebe 57
Mendenhall, Absolom 13
  Hannah 7
  William 12
  Wm. 30
Menson, Isaac A. 51
Merchant, Smith 17
Meredith, Nancy 29
Merret, William 10
Merrian, Christopher 17
Merrick, Henry 11
  Rachel 15
Mewman, Wm. 44
Michael, Wm. 27
Mickell, Molly 3
Middlelin, Polly 23
Middleton, J. 27
  L. 17
  Mary 57
  Nancy 56
  Nice 18
  Smallwood 36
  William 22
Midget, Peggy 26
Miles, Isaac 22
  M. A. J. 58
Milikan, Matilda 48
Miller, Abraham 58
  Ann 40
  Catherine 42
  Elizabeth 54, 58
  Geo. 43
  Hansey 1
  Isaac A. 44
  Jacob 12, 23
  Jane 49
  Jannie 26
  John 11, 19, 47, 55
  Jonathan (see Milles)
  Joseph 23
  Julian 56
  Lavinca 34
  Lissa 59
  Margaret 19
  Mary 3, 9, 50
  Polly 32
  Sally 29
  Susannah 24
  Wm. H. 40
Milles, Elizabeth 9

Milles (cont.)
  Jane 34
  Jonathan (Miller) 18
  Mary 3
  Moses B. 47
  Russel 38
Millikan, Eda 48
Milliken, Elihu 18
  Henry 38
  James 39
  William 2
  Wm. 23
Mills, Aaron 25
  Alice 42
  C. 27
  Catherine 11
  Charity 20
  Eli 27
  Elijah 38
  Elizabeth 49
  Hannah 34, 41
  Hugh 37
  James 31
  Jesse 31
  John 2, 36, 44, 46
  Jonathan 31
  Joseph 8
  Josiah 47
  Lidia 50
  Lydia 39
  M. 17
  Martha 32
  Mary 32, 39
  Moses 22
  Nancy 22
  Nathan 30
  Patsy 36
  Priscilla 47
  Rachel 24
  Rebecca 24
  Reuben 14
  Robert C. 42, 51
  Ruthy 28
  S. 17
  Solomon 44
  Thomas 19
  Thomas T. 51
  Wm. 7, 25, 31, 34, 35, 52
  Z. 27
  Zachariah 7
Minick, John 40
Minger, Stony 40
Minut, Susannah 27
Mitchell, John 23
  Baxton 25

Mitchell (cont.)
  Berry 19, 55
  James 35
  John 16
  Jopp 53
  N. 7
  Nancy 16
  Penelope 55
  Samuel 58
  Willie 51
  Wm. M. 55
Modrell, Nina 3
Moffett, John 2, 18
  Wm. D. 53
  Wm. H. 50
Molden, Elizabeth 19
  Valentine 6
Molsby, Ann 2
  Elinor 12
Monos, Amos 44
Monroe, Nancy 33
Monut, Elenor 48
Mooney, Joseph 12
Mooser, Eliza 33
Mopson, John 37
Moree, Sally 53
Moreland, Thomas 35
Morgan, Hannah 22
  Hezekiah 28
  John 4
  Levi 35
  Lucy 4
  Nancy 4
  Rhoda 53
  Robert 37
Morrison, Wm. 33
Morrow, Carolina M. H. 44
  David 8
  Eliza D. 40
  Martha Jane C. 50
  Priscilla 41
  Wm. T. 43
Moser, Francis 33
  Nancy 39
  Wm. 33
Mosier, Rachel 37
Mosses, Julian 35
Mount, Betsey 32
  John 23, 36
  Mary 48
  Polly 31
  Wm. T. 56
Moyer, Christopher 35
Mozier, Catharine A. 52
Montgomery, Anne 8

Montgomery (cont.)
  John 7
  Michael 9
  Wm. 6
  Wm. A. 30
Moore, Alex 58
  Ann 2
  Anny 22
  Betsy 23
  Chaney 21
  Cinthia 55
  David 4
  Dorcas 58
  E. 40
  Ealbey 28
  Eleanor 48
  Elender 58
  Elijah 26, 41
  Elisha 26
  Ephram 24
  Fanny 3, 14, 22
  George 37
  Hannah B. 38
  Isaac 32
  James 25
  Jane 14
  Jesse 4, 16, 20, 21
  John 14, 29, 44, 53
  John H. 17
  Joseph 20
  Joshua 22
  K. 33
  Latin 39
  Louisa 56
  Malinda 18
  Martha 14
  Mary Jane W. 41
  Nancy 5
  Patty 11
  Peggy 26
  Polly 21, 47, 52
  Rachel 5
  Ruth 6
  S. 10
  Sallie 15
  Sally 14, 28
  Sarah 33
  Scynthia 28
  Seth 3
  Stephen 33
  Susannah 21, 29
  Thomas 24
  Thos. J. 55
  Wm. 7, 26, 30
Morris, Ann 8

Morris (cont.)
  Betsy 9
  Charlotte 55
  Elizabeth 43
  Hannah 26
  James 30
  John 21, 22
  Nancy 8
  Patrick 3
  Peggy 2
  S. C. 55
  Sarah 59
  Vina 53
  Wm. 54
Moyers, David 5
  Elizabeth 16, 37
  Grizzy 23
  James B. 38
  John 54
  John (see Myers)
  Joshua (see Mayers)
  Polly 23
  Wm. 38
Mudkipp, Kimble 27
Mullins, D. 47
  Joel 31
  Nancy 30
Mundenhall, Stephen 9
  Susannah 29
Munick, Ruthy 27
Murphy, Daniel R. 35
  Lena 1
  M. 42
  Nancy 17
  Sarah 40
  William 18
Murray, Sallie 17
Murry, Charity 4
Music, Polly 33
Myers, Alfred J. 51
  George W. 41
  Henry H. 33
  Hiram 52
  John 4
  John (Moyers) 22
  Margaret 50
  Mary D. 52
  Sally 4
  Susannah 4, 24
  Wm. 54
Mynat, Susan 51
Mynatt, Harriet 57
Myrick, Rebecca 42
Myuck, John 36
Nail, Elizabeth 26

Nance, Clement 26
  Nancy 15
  Peggy 26
Nanney, Margaret 45
Naples, Wilson 50
Nation, Charity 11
  Edward 8
  Sampson 5
  Thomas 21
Neal, Benj. 40, 54
  Charles 5
  Dice 43
  Elizabeth 35
  James L. 35
  Jeremiah 17, 26
  Leah 20
  Leonne 5
  Mary 53
  Patsy 58
  Rebecca 59
Neas, Thomas 48
Neeley, Andrew 23
  Ann 11
  James 16
  Patsy 8
  Rosannah 16
Neely, John 15
  Paggy 25
  Polly 11
Neil, David 7
  William 17
  Wm. 6
Neile, Mary 2
Neilson, John 4
Nelson, James 31
  John 17
  Jonathan 59
  Joshua 30
  Lewis 39
  Lucinda 52
  Mary Ann 35
  Thomas 38, 49
  Wm. 3
Nenner, Catharine 28
Nenney, Mary G. 41
Nenny, Lydia 38
Netherton, E. 4
Neugin, Thomas 23
Newman, Aaron 38, 59
  Alexander 27
  Betsy 28, 33, 57
  Blair 30
  Catherine 53, 59
  Edward 44
  Elizabeth 50, 51

Newman (cont.)
  Geo. W. 57
  Isaac 19
  Isaac M. 44
  James 35
  James G. 44
  Jared 10
  Jno. 59
  John 29, 36, 51
  John N. 35
  Jonathan 25
  Joseph 8
  Joshua 20
  Madison 58
  Margaret 47
  Mary E. 34
  Melissa 44
  Polly 29, 33
  Rebecca 7, 13, 39
  Sally 34
  Samuel 12
  Samuel T. 54
  Sarah 32, 40
  Thomas J. 53
  William C. H. 58
Newton, Nancy 56
  Sophia W. 42
Nichalson, Catherine 41
Nicholas, Matilda 48
Nicholason, Ruth 58
Nichols, Judith 3
Nicholson, Jeremiah 8
  Joseph 13
Nickles, George 8
Niel, Elizabeth 8
  Thomas 5
Night, Caroline 54
  Richard 42
  Thomas 42
Nitchell, Mary 46
Noah, John 28
Noland, Daniel 47
Nolley, Joseph M. 54
Noore, Robert 48
Norman, Jesse 34
North, Elizabeth 57
  James 35
  Mary 52
  Peter 42, 50
Northern, Nancy 29
  W. T. 23
  Wm. 29
Norwood, John 28
Noun, H. 50
Nount, Sarah 48

Pearce (cont.)
  Hannah 21
  Thomas 21
Pearson, John 31
  Margaret 36
  Polly 30
Peasland, Martha 46
Peay, Jno. (see Reay)
Peck, Adam 28
  Benj. 16, 27
  Betsey 39
  Eliza 28
  Eliza Jane 53
  Eliza S. 49
  Elizabeth 31, 41
  Elliott 18
  Henry H. 30
  Jacob 20
  Jenny 15
  John 41
  John H. 49
  Juliet 56
  L. A. 57
  Manah L. S. 49
  Sarah 35
  Susannah 34
Peek, Polly 24
Peerman, John 37
Pegmore, Darkie (Prigmore) 11
Pendill, Ann 10
Pendleton, Sally 30
Penketon, Obadiah 43
Penkslow, M. L. 34
Penn, Rebecca 10
Perdy, Dianna 10
Perkins, Francis 34
  Judah 19
Perkupile, Nancy 27
Pernonat, Elizabeth 12
Perrian, William 14
Perriman, Jno. 20
Perrin, Vaden 43
Perrine, Methew 12
Perrion, Polly 47
Perry, Delilah 22
  Mary 1
Peton, John 18
Petty, John 6, 7
  Polly 27
  Samuel 51
  William 7
Phagan, James 20
Phelan, Jesse 43
Pheniz, Mathew 5
Phillips, Elizabeth 50

Phillips (cont.)
  John 42
  Margaret 40
  Marry 45
  Rebecca 19
Pickens, John 11
Pierce, Albert 50
  Caleb 16
  Cobb 54
  David 20, 60
  Geo. 43
  Hannah 17
  James 37
  Jonathan 59
  Rachel 53
Pigg, Elizabeth 44
Pite, Elizabeth 58
Pitts, Louisa 52
Pogne, John 47
Poindexter, B. 8
  Parthena 58
Polak, Nancy 47
Pollard, James 47
  Stephen 48
  Thomas 48
Pollock, Elizabeth Ann 38
  Margaret 43
Pope, Hannah 15
  Mary Ann 47
  William 8
Potter, Jeffries 4
Potters, Lucy 3
Prackett, Jno. 23
Prater, Benjamine 5
Pratt, Rebecca 8
Preddy, B. (see Priddy)
  Elizabeth 12
Presly, Sylvanna 53
Prewit, Elisha 31
  Wm. 30
Prewitt, James 19
  John 20, 22
  Martha 20
  Sally 16
Price, Millie 27, 27
  Zimly 59
Prichard, Lidia 29
Priddy, B. (Preddy) 21
  Polly 14
Prigmore, Darkie (see Pegmore)
  Elizabeth (see Pugmoor)
  Lydia (see Pugmore)
Prince, Solomon 23
Privett, Rebecca 13
Province, Oliver 38

Provine, Wm. 1
Pruet, Wm. 57
Pruit, Polly 4
Prukepile, Reuben 33
Pucket, Jane 26
  Patsy 20
Puckett, Allen 20
  Douglass 14
  Francis 46
  Nancy 35
Pugmoor, Elizabeth (Prigmore) 8
Pugmore, Lydia (Prigmore) 19
Pullen, Wiley 59
Pulliam, Penelope 59
Pullins, Martha 39
Pulse, Frederick 23
  Geo. W. 40
  George W. 28
Punkey, Susannah 37
Purkepile, Reuben 33
Purkpile, Isaac 51
Putman, Betsy 35
  Jenny 39
Putner, Nancy 30
Quarles, Mary Ann 32
Quarrles, Peggy 41
Quarrillion, James 52
Quarrells, Margaret 47
Quolls, Fanny 32
Rach, Daniel 39
Rader, Elizabeth 58
Rains, George 9
Ralbertt, Ross (Talbott) 37
Ramsey, Eleanor 51
  James 51
  Jno. 19
  Robert 15
  Samuel 14
  Zilpha 57
Randolph, Elizabeth 13, 46
  Henry 4, 51
  Lucy 5
  Mary 17, 56
  Patsy 50
  Sallie 17
  Susannah 23
Randols, Sally 37
Rankin, _____ 5
  Catherine 59
  Christopher 55
  David 25
  Elizabeth 36
  Isabella 14, 22, 35
  J. D. 51
  Jane A. 50

Rankin (cont.)
  John 26
  Nancy 5, 57
  Samuel 40
  Sarah 35, 45
  Sinai 38
  Thomas 30, 33
  Thomas C. 47
  William 59
Raulstone, James 10
  Moses 11
  Samuel 10
Rawlings, Elizabeth 52
Ray, George 4
  John 8
Rayl, Desdemons 59
  George 30
Rea, Martha M. 45
Reach, Hannah 54
Read, Jno. (see Reay)
Readsno, Thomas 4
Reams, Daniel 42
  Elizabeth 40
  John 6
  Sarah 27
Reaves, Samuel 26
Reay, Jno. (Peay)(Read) 20
Reddin, Mordica 21
Reece, Elizabeth 59
  Polly 27
  Rachel 21
Reed, Elijah 38
  Eliza Ann 45
  Jean 2
  Jesse T. 60
  John 19
  Permelia 29
  Robert 4, 16
  Sally 60
  Samuel 54
  Sarah 18
Reeder, Betsy 19
Reedy, Elizabeth 1
Reems, Richard D. 40
Reese, David 26
  Emly G. 44
  Garrett 14
  Julia A. 24
  Peggy 28, 34
Reeves, James 27
  Nancy 19
  Sarah 55
Reid, Thomas 33
Renean, Isaac 44
Reneau, George 24

Reneau (cont.)
Guley 29
Hezekiah 24
M. 36
Mary 8
Preston 52
Wm. 56
Renfro, John 55
Renne, Peggy 2
Rennels, William 17
Renno, Barley 5
Cisse 9
Elizabeth 15
F. 27
George 2
John 9
Polly 16
Rentfro, Sally 2
Reppetoe, James 45
Reynold, Martha 46
Reynolds, Charlotte 51
Hiram 35
Lydia 40
Rhea, Florence 45
Rheams, Jane 51
Rhineheart, Polly 31
Rhoton, John F. 56
Rian, Wm. 42
Rice, Augustus 34
John G. W. 41
Lewellan 44
Polly 21
Thomas 52
Wm. 38
Richey, Elizabeth 45
Ricket, Joanna 35
Rickets, Abel 34
John 28
Rickett, Elizabeth 59
Ricketts, Elizabeth 18
Riddle, Elizabeth 48
Hohanna 48
Jeremiah 7
Susan 45
Zachariah 3
Riddler, Stephen 4
Riggins, Orena 58
Riggs, Arobel 53
Azarah 38
Casandra 13
Emaline 59
Harvey 47
Jesse 34, 44
John 38
Nancy 14, 19, 24

Riggs (cont.)
Phebe 34
Polly 23
Samuel 38
Wm. 11
Zadock 29
Right, Nancy 24
Rightsell, John 19
Rightwell, George 59
Riley, Jeremiah 23
Nancy 47
Rinehart, Betsy 50
John 43
Phillip 19
Sally 27
Riot, Barnabas 57
Rippetoe, Fanny 40
James 46
Washington 40
Willis 45, 46
Ritchey, Alexander 7
Betsy D. 33
Hannah 33
Isabella 4
John 31, 32, 34
Nancy 24
Nathaniel D. 35
Peggy 17
Robt. 34
Thomas 35
Ritchie, James 23
Ritter, Averritt 35
Eliza 41
Roach, Susannah 12
Roak, Mary 20
Robard, Nancy 26
Roberson, Jesse 47
Roberton, V. 6
Roberts, Catherine 24
Isham 25
John 5
Moses 31
Robertson, Axey 33
Benjamine 52
Eliza 39
Elizabeth 17
Jezekiah 57
John 29, 45
Nancy 30
Robeson, John 45
Robinson, Anna 27
Betsy 16
James 33
John 22, 44, 46
Matthew 59

Robinson (cont.)
  Polly 15
  Susannah 11
  Thomas 21
Rodden, Robert 28
Roddick, Thomas 26
Roddy, Anna 14
  Isaac 34
  John 26
  Sidnah 31
  Thos. 38
Roddye, Bridget 6
  Jesse 5
  Rachel 6
  Sarah 9
Rodgers, Alexr. 18
  Isaac 27, 34
  Jacob 32
  Jenny 27
  Lucy 24
  Martha 31
  Polly (Hodges) 21
  Polly (see Rogers)
  Sallie 39
  Sally 27
Rogers, Ann 1
  Dorcas A. 55
  Elisha 55
  Elizabeth 59
  Jane 27, 42
  John 7, 43
  Letty 21
  Martha 4
  Polly (Rodgers) 21
  Rhoda C. 48
  Tabitha 39
  Thomas 5
Rolin, Sarah 4
Rollins, Robert 57
Rolston, Sally 27
Romine, Mary 57
Romines, L. 26
Rooy, Charles 26
Roper, Joseph 17
  Mary Ann 34
Roran, Tabitha 11
Rorex, John 12
Roulstone, Elizabeth 1
  William 2
Roupe, George 29
Routh, Ester 8
  Geo. W. 59
  Jane 41
  John 14, 48
  Jonathan 42

Routh (cont.)
  Mary 53
  Nancy 36
  Rosahah 44
  Wm. 11
Rowen, Robert 25
Rowland, George 30
Rowx, Dave 6
Royal, Nancy 14
Royer, John 29
  Polly 30
Royers, Rolin 22
Royl, Delana 48
Royston, Peggy 28
Ruble, Peter 43
Rucker, John 6
Rugh, James 44
Runnean, Freeman 5
Russel, Florence 3
  James 8
Russell, Anna 34
  B. 15
  David 19
  Elizabeth 36
  Ellis 1
  George 55
  George W. 29
  Hiram 34
  John 30
  Lewes 10
  Lucinda 45
  Mary 3
  Peggy 3
  Peter 43
  Rachel 7, 55
  Rachel H. 47
  Rebecca 7
  Sallie 15
  Thomas 31, 53
Ruth, Isaac 16
  Nancy 41
  Solomon 41
Rutherford, Joseph 56
Ryans, Allison 55
  Peggy (see Hyans)
Saffield, Samuel 10
Sage, Nancy 49
Salton, John A. 55
Salvage, William 10
Samith, Barton 28
Samples, Amy 6
  Hannah 34
  Nancy 4
  Ruth 1
  William 2

Sampson, Elijah 45
  James 39
  Julianna 32
  Lucinda 38
  M. 33
  Matilda 43
  Polly 16
Sanders, Nancy 39
Sandusky, Rosanna 5
Sarrete, Allen 31
Sartain, John 58
  Mary 58
  Wm. 33
Sartin, Dorcas 39
  James 39
  John 40
  T. 45, 46
Sartion, Elizabeth 45
Sarton, Jenny (Barton) 31
Sasseen, Elizabeth 42
Sassern, Frankie 28
Satterfield, George G. 32
  Levi 53
Saunders, Frederick 9
  Jual 23
  Richard 22
Sawett, Thomas 28
Scaggs, Anna M. 60
Scarlett, Stephen 47
Scheckels, Rutha 50
Scipe, Polly 33
Scoke, Rebecca 20
  Scott, Andrew 25
  Eleanor 18
  Isabella 3
  Polly Ann 32
  Robert H. 56
  Robt. A. 31
Scribner, James 33
  Jno. 54
Scruggs, Frederick 54
  Henry 55
  Miles F. 58
Seabourne, Joseph 6
Seahorn, Alexander 36
  Catherine 10
  George 25
  Jenny 16
  John, Jr. 7
  Levice 10
  Margaret 58
Seal, Thomas 40
Sehorn, Hugh 28
  Jacob 9, 20
  Mahaley 14

Self, Job 14
Selfhennir, Polly 25
Sellars, Edward 30
  Mary 30
Sellers, John 41, 50
  Hannah 27
  Mary 20
  Nathan 24
  Patsy 16
  Peggy 20
  Thomas 41
  Wm. 41
Selvege, Henry 27
Selvidge, Eleanor 31
Semrell, Narcissa 38
Sevier, Phillip 9
Sewell, George 18
  Susannah 27
Shadden, Isabella 24
  Nancy 8
  Peggy 21
  Polly 14, 26
  Thomas 3
  William 8
  Wilson 59
Shanks, Ann 1
  Ruth 22
Shannon, John 19
  Wm. 42, 42
Sharp, Jane 17
  Jenny 30
  Mary 2
  Turner 49
Shaw, David 37
Sheddan, Elizabeth 14
  Joseph 14
  Peggy 14
Shedden, Joseph 45
Sheek, Nancy 12
Shelley, Nathan 29
  Penelope 57
Shellin, Thomas 24
Shelly, Abby 25
  Dorothy 51
  Elizabeth 7
  James 43
  Mary 51
  Nathan, Jr. 20
  Polly 13
Shelton, Ann 1
  Eli 25
  Ellender 6
  James 27
  Polly 8
  Turman 11

Snodgrass, Amanda 41
   David 8
   Elizabeth 15
   Elizabeth R. 52
   Isaac 35
   Jane 16
   John 10
   Margery 14
   Mary 2
   Robert 4
Snolly, Abner (see Snoddy)
Snow, James 19
   Jennie 27
   Pleasant 47
Soliman, Elizabeth 2
Solimon, Abraham 25
   Eda 10
   James 20
Solomon, Susan 7
Southerland, John 24
   Wm. 57
Spangler, Devota 21
   Mary 13
   Polly 7
   Rebecca 17
Sparker, Thomas 27
Sparks, Betsey 55
   Leonard 15
Spice, Susannah 49
Spoon, Susannah 32
Springer, Edward 7
Squires, John 46
Stafford, Sallie 9
Stamith, Henry (Smith) 44
Stanback, Mary (Stanbuck) 20
Stanbuck, Mary (see Stanback)
Stanley, Jonna 21
Stansberry, Wm. 24
Staples, Catharine 34
   Francis 27
   James 37
   John 37
   John G. 35
   Kittie 25
   Margaret 59
   Mecha 53
   Peggy 15
   Richard 29
Starr, Sampson 60
Steard, Sessan 30
Stedman, Rebecca 16
Steele, W. H. 53
Stephen, Annie 16
Stephens, David 4
   Edward 10

Stephens (cont.)
   Margaret 53
Stephenson, Catherine 40
   Edward 6
   Eliza 57
   Elizabeth 32
   Robert 13
   Sara 22
   Silas B. 34
Sterling, John 39
   Katherine 2
   Margaret 2
   Mary 7
   Polly 7
Steward, Polly 21
Stewart, William 8
Stiff, Edward 37
   Nancy 46
Still, A. 3
Stilwell, Rebecca 8
Stinett, Preston 44
Stone, Allen 34
   Mary 49
Stoples, Mary 40
Storm, Jacob 21
Stringfield, Thomas 41
Stropea, Charles 15
Stropes, Abraham 22
Stroud, Thomas 52
Stuart, Henry 38
Strupes, Christiana 17
Stubbleffeld, Rebecca 29
Stubblefield, James 34
   Mary 33
   Raleigh 56
   Wesley 48
Sullens, Nancy 17
Sullins, Joseph 3
Sullivan, Margaret 3
Sumers, Rebecca 31
Summers, Betsey 56
   L. 46
   Manning 48
   Vena 47
   W. 41
Summitt, T. 58
Summon, Wm. R. 55
Summons, Sally 38
Sunderland, Edna 55
   Mary 39, 52
Surrate, Samuel 43
Surratt, Nancy 54
Sutherland, Abraham 11
   Andrew 5
   Betsy 11

Sutherland (cont.)
Elender 17
Elizabeth 4
Phillip 16
Rachel 23
Rebecca 24
Sarah 12
Susannah 16
Tenna 17
Sutliff, James 32, 33
Nancy 32
Sutton, P. 20
Swain, Lidie (see Swann)
Swainey, Patty 5
Swan, Margaret 32
Swann, Leah L. 60
Lidie (Swain) 22
Polly 27
Robt. 25
Susan 44
Swingle, Catherine 10
Swniney, John Allen 15
Sallie 15
Syms, Jennie 10
Taafe, Peter 17
Tackett, Peter 14
Taff, Elizabeth 26, 40, 50
James 28
Jesse 40
John 28
Peter 34
Rachel 22
Wm. 29
Tague, Hezekiah 44
Mathes (Teague) 36
Taland, Arsena 56
Talbot, Letitia 56
Sarah 36
Talbott, Elizabeth 22, 35
James 58
Joseph 27
Ross (see Ralbertt)
Sophia 20
Tallant, Polly 39
Talley, Dudley 6
Tally, A. C. 59
Beverly 60
Joseph 38
Tankersley, Eliza 59
Reuben 56
Tanner, James B. 59
Rachel 51
Rhoda 10
Tarwater, Jacob 4
Tate, Wm. 14

Taylor, A. 14
Elizabeth 24, 30, 55
Greenberry 17
James 42
Jno. E. 18
Joseph 53
Lemal 13
Leroy 19
Levice 28
Lewes 8
Malinda 49
Manala 26
Margaret 34
Mary alias Polly 12
Mathilda 14
Polly 28
R. 12
Rachel 16
Sarah 11
Wm. 29, 30
Teague, Mathes (see Tague)
Templar, Moses 10
Templeton, Edward 18
Wm. 42
Teney, Polly 10
Terrill, Betsey 24
Thames, Amos 20
Thammins, Edward 24
Tharp, Nancy 32
Sallie 22
Thomas, Abrahan 49
Ann 59
Antepas 14
C. 28
David 34
Elizabeth 38
Henry 31
Jacob 38
James 59
Jane 17
Jas. 39
Joseph 1
Lydia 33
Nancy 32, 58
Peter 30
Polly 24
Reuben 28, 37
Rosannah 33
Sally 23
Unice 50
Thompson, Alexander 9
Allen 3
Baxter 47
Betsey 29
Delila 51

Thompson (cont.)
  Elisa 29
  Isaac L. J. 36
  Joseph 1
  Nathan 2
  Samuel 46
  Susannah 13
  Washington 46
  Wm. 31
Thompston, Jacob G. 54
Thornbrough, Abigail 12
  Amos 11
  Richard 12
  W. 13
Thornburg, John 24
  Lavinia 32
  Sophia 7
Thornburgh, A. 28
  Aly 27
  Anne 29
  Charity 17
  Elizabeth 22, 36
  Henry 2
  Jane L. 59
  Joel 10
  Jonathan 25
  Lydia 27
  Mary 17, 31
  Minnard 45
  Morgan 9
  Obed C. 47
  Phebe 41
  Rachel 41
  Richard 13
  Wm. 28, 35, 44
Thornhill, Anne L. 50
  Betsy 38
  Joseph 49
  Richard 40
  Mary 48
Thornton, Eliza 46
  Rebecca 42
  Clark 1
  David 20
  Lydia 32
Thorton, Lettice 7
Tillny, Molly 1
Timmons, Solomon 54
Tipton, Joseph 3
  Lavina 18
Toale, Nancy 59
Todd, Anna 33
  Dandridge 25
  Hiram 56
  Isaac 26

Todd (cont.)
  James 24
  L. 5
  Martha 59
  Nancy 31
  Samuel 11
Tollaver, Zachary 47
Tolls, Stokley 30
Tools, Levna 54
Toungn, John 27
Traglen, Lavina 49
Trammon, Peter 11
Travis, Phillip 59
Treadway, Elizabeth 48
Treviathan, William 17
Trevillion, C. 54
  John T. 49
  William 56
Trott, Wm. 57
Trotter, Isabelle 6
Trotts, Wm. 53
Trustly, Hyran 46
Tsevillion, Joab 45
Tucker, Elizabeth 22
  John 32
  Judith 10
  Levinia 11
  Nancy 6
  Thomas 54
  Wiley 13
Tunley, Mary 28
Turk, James 33
Turman, Mina 3
Turner, Amee 20
  Annie 15
  Charlotte (Lewis) 59
  Dorothy 5
  Elizabeth 5
  Henry 41
  James 43
  Jemina 14
  John 32
  Margaret 52
  Mary 49
  Nathan 21
  Richard 38
  Robert 4
  Royal 43
  William 18
Twinney, Nancy 16
Tyans, Wm. 57
Tyler, Betsey 58
  Elizabeth 56
  Phelik 48
  Sarah 48

Underwood, Elizabeth 39
  Mahala 48
  Margaret 40
  Preston 51
  Sally 44
  Susannah 32
Ursary, Diana 54
Ursey, John 52
Vance, David 12, 34
  Jane 28
  Mary 51
  Robert 35, 40
  Sarah 4
  Wm. 16
Vandike, Mary 34
Vandyke, Elizabeth 26
  Henry 34
  Richard W. 55, 55
Vanhooser, Delilah 16
  Jacob 16
  John 12, 52
  Thomas 41
  Valentine 52
Vanhoun, Rachel 6
Varnelle, Priscilla 51
Vineyard, Wm. 29
Voiles, Levi 44
Voss, Thomas D. 54
Waddle, George 1
Walder, Nancy 6
Walker, Andrew 40
  Daniel 45
  Elinor 8
  Elizabeth 17, 48
  Ellis 59
  Francis 19
  George 26
  Haynes 56
  Henry (see Wilkes)
  Jacob 48
  James 15, 26
  Jane 16
  Jean 1
  Jenny 3
  Jeremiah 24, 42, 57
  John 40
  Mary 37
  Milly 31
  Nancy 47
  Osborne R. 49
  Patsey 30
  Patsy 48
  Polly 24
  Polly Ann 45
  Sally 50

Walker (cont.)
  Sophia 18
  Susannah 19, 36
  Thomas 11
  Wm. 27, 51, 53
Wall, Wadlington 28
Wallace, Mary R. 55
  Oliver 3
  Pulaski 21
Walter, Juda 43
  Wm. 25
Walters, George 21
  Sallie 27
Walton, Matilda 34
  Nancy 40, 58
Ward, Alfa 58
  Ann 36
  B. 58
  Betsy 38
  James 35
  Jonathan S. 57
  L. 30
  Mary 3
  Mary B. 53
  Obadiah 49
  Pheobe 54
  Rachael 3
  Sally 25
Warmon, Barbara 17
Watkins, Araminta 36
  Eliza G. 42
  Elizabeth 25
  G. 33
  Isaac I. 28
  Joel 7
  John 40
  Margaret 29
  Philip 30
  Sarah 57
  Wm. 28, 53
Watson, Andrew 37
Watts, J. 50
Weaver, Barbara 9
  Elizabeth 2, 40
  Mary 33
  Susannah 9
Webb, Ben 53
  Centy 12
  Jennena 22
  John 3
  Mary 21, 58
  Nancy 54
  Richard 12
  Wm. 22
Weden, Geo. 52

Williams (cont.)
Sally 31
Samuel 47
Sarah 41
Susannah 9, 18
Thomas 9, 12, 15
Wm. U. 27
Williford, Merrida 56
Wm. 54
Willis, Isarel 18
John 22
Willongskley, Enoch 24
Willoughby, M. B. 56
Polly 23
Susannah 52
Wills, Zebedel 40
Wilmott, James 36
Wilmouth, Patsy 36
Wilson, Abel 28
Amos 49
Benj. W. 40
David 8
Elinor 6
Elizabeth 55
Ely 32
Emeline 56
Hannah 20
Isaac 8
Isaac H. 46
James 51
John 6
Lydia 20
Mary 3
Mary Ann 53
Nancy 13
Nollie 6
Peggy 16
Polly 49
Rachel 20
Robert J. 39
Vinie 48
William 10
Wm. 26
Wm. M. 35
Winterbowers, Elizabeth 20
Winters, Margaret 43
Wise, Benj. 58
James 40
Joseph 58
Nancy 25
Simon 24
Wiseman, Nancy 33
Wistly, Polly 23
Witt, Andrew 52
Annie 15

Witt (cont.)
Betsey 2
Catherine 57
David 24
Eli 15
Elijah 5
Elizabeth 11, 44
Elvira L. 57
Enoch 25
H. 16
James 25, 50
John 19
John S. 45
Joseph 4, 49
Mary 16
Nancy 39
Nathaniel 13
Noah 2, 30
P. 25
Sally 30
Sarah 20
Silas 23
Wilson C. 60
Wm. 45
Wolf, John 33
Wolly, Solomon 39
Wood, Ann 12
Elizabeth 8, 14, 38
F. 6
I. C. 51
James 16
Jonathan 42
Polly P. 34
William 22
Woodall, Nancy 17
Woodard, Ann 27
Jean 2
Mary 24
Samuel 25
Woodert, Jno. 3
Woods, Elizabeth 46
Geo. W. 14
H. M. 41
James 43
Jas. B. 35
Jefferson 41
Joel 20
John 33
John G. M. 52
Joseph 33
Michael 11
Nancy 49
Richard 2
Sarah 52
Wiley, Jr. 28

Woodward, Anna 41
  Aylse 7
  Eliza 5
  Jesse 53
Wooten, Betsy 58
  Joseph 54
  Sally 52
Worley, Betsy 57
  Joseph 57
  Nancy 51
Worly, Susannah 32
Wormsley, Sarah J. 51
Wray, Catherine 34
  George 34
Wright, David 47
  James 6, 16
  John 33, 55

Wright (cont.)
  Nathan 3
  Polly 1, 5
  Wm. 50
Wyatt, Mary 37
  Thomas 7
  Wm. 58
Yates, Sarah H. 50
Yeager, Nicholas 15
Yoken, Solimon 1
York, Simon 12
Young, Betsy 31
  Francis 40
  Jesse 44
  Josiah 48
  Nathaniel 39

ADDENDA

Branner, Christiana 43   Small, Sarah 8

www.ingramcontent.com/pod-product-compliance
Lightning Source LLC
Chambersburg PA
CBHW070255290326
41930CB00041B/2529